IMAGES
of America

FALCON FIELD

Falcon Field was created to train British Royal Air Force pilots for duty in World War II. Because of this program, and the sacrifices made by local residents and members of the Allied military forces (24 of the 54 cadets from Course 10, pictured here, paid the ultimate price), Mesa, Arizona, has one the busiest municipal airports in the world and a thriving business community surrounding it. (Courtesy of Catherine Hutchin Harris.)

On the Cover: Taken in the mid-1950s, this image offers a glimpse into the sense of community the employees of the businesses in and around Falcon Field Airport had after working together to train British and American cadets to fly in World War II. (Courtesy of Falcon Field Airport, City of Mesa.)

IMAGES
of America

FALCON FIELD

Daryl F. Mallett

ISBN 978-0-7385-7137-9

Published by Arcadia Publishing
Charleston, South Carolina

Printed in the United States of America

Library of Congress Control Number: 2008941568

For all general information contact Arcadia Publishing at:
Telephone 843-853-2070
Fax 843-853-0044
E-mail sales@arcadiapublishing.com
For customer service and orders:
Toll-Free 1-888-313-2665

Visit us on the Internet at www.arcadiapublishing.com

For my dear wife, Barbara, and my beautiful children, Jacob, Christian, and Maia Mallett. Without you, this journey would be empty. For Rex Griswold. Your love of history made this possible. And for the men and women who trained and worked at Falcon Field and the world, some of whom paid the ultimate price. Thank you for preserving a world in which this book could be written.

CONTENTS

ACKNOWLEDGMENTS

Prior to when I covered for a local newspaper the story of Falcon's Fox Studio swimming pool being demolished, I didn't know British cadets trained in Mesa, or that my favorite starlet, Gene Tierney, shot a movie here. How little did I realize the truth in his words when Jim Dawson, author of *The RAF in Arizona: Falcon Field, 1941–1945*, wrote, "Be careful. We might get you seriously hooked on Falcon history!" and enclosed a photograph of Tierney at Falcon.

History is never written alone, and this book is due to the assistance of the people here with thanks especially to Ken Beeby, Jodey Elsner, Jane Eppinga, Joan Franks Gannon, Phillip Goorian, Rex Griswold, Connie Gullatt-Whiteman, Catherine Hutchin Harris, Jackie Leyva, Carolyn Wischler McDaniel, Molly Turner, and Ruth Wischler.

Thanks to individuals from various organizations: Roc Arnett, Eddie Basha, Jeff Bassett, Ray Berg, David Lawrence Boutros, Helen Brown, Cindy Bush, Julie Clark, Natalia Cody, Bobbye Jo Coke, Amanda Covington, Jack Crandall, Bernice Cuisinier, Susan and Rich Cutshall, Layna Dechant, Peter Duchin, Lisa Dunbar, Jim Edwards, Rita Erickson, Roberta Esch, Art Fiacco, Gwen Florea, Sarge Glenn, Brooke Hayward, Scott Heideman, Drew Henschen, Jerry Howard, Rob Johnson, Eric Jones, Lynda Jordan, Hal Klopper, Jay Larscheid, Jim Law, Margaret MacMinn-Barton, Ramon Martinez, Catherine May, Cindy McGown, Hugh McSpadden, Hassan Mirza, Yvonne Morris, Tom Nicoud, Sandy and Veronica Novelli, Corrine Nystrom, Carl Olander, Melissa Randazzo, Gloria Rico, Lori Roberts, Jami Savage, Gordon Shirling, Anne Selleck, Larry Simmons, Melanie Slocum, Jared Smith, Anne Stackpole, James Stemm, Mark Stevens, Floyd Stilwell, Dennis and Terri Teten, Carole Thompson-Sutton, Barrett Tillman, Larry Turner, Anna Uremovich, Elizabeth Walsh, Lois Yates, J&J Materials, and the Orson Pratt Brown Family Organization.

Thanks to the No 4. British Flying Training School and RAF family members Roger Amundson, Tom Austin, Mary Louise Bustrin, Ray Corn, Dan Darnell, Horace Griffen, Eric Grimster, Frank Horner, Wally Martin, Bill McCash, Carl Scott, and Mark Swope.

Local families who helped are Alice Boyle, Art Freeman, Mary Habeeb, Janet and Virginia Ikeda, Sadie Ishikawa, Bobby Jordan, Robin Juvan, Wayne McKellips, Ralph Pew, Wayne Pomeroy, C. K. Sato, Otto Shill, Don Strauch, and Marge Reiner Thayer.

Friends include Meg Allen, Cody Barker, Devon Brown, Mary Burgess, Howard Carrillo, Angela Miller Caudill, Mark Crockett, Carole and Shannon Dempsey, Sam and Trude Duckworth, Mark Goldstein, Darin and Reagan Guthrie, Heather Houston, Hans Kugler, Brendan Maclear, Kelly McCray, Ethan Moe, David Myers, Rob Reginald, George and Dani Slusser, Bridget Stoll, Malinda and Cammie Terry, James Douglas True, Scott Vaughn, Troy Walker, and Liz Warren.

Thanks also to my family: Bill and Masuko Mallett; David, Stacie, Jonathan, and Victoria Gonzales; Brianna Valdez; Rick Gray; Brad, Sherry, Tricia, Stephen, and Catherine Biggs; Thad, Annette, Andrew, and Megan Aylsworth; and my wife, Barbara, and children, Jacob, Christian, and Maia Mallett, for love and inspiration every day.

INTRODUCTION

Agriculture has always been big business in Arizona and specifically in Mesa. The Hohokam Indians, who occupied the area from Flagstaff, Arizona, to the Mexican border, had built a system of canals stretching 125 miles, and the Salt River flowed through what is now Mesa. When the Mormon settlers arrived in the late 1870s, they rejuvenated some of the canals for their agricultural needs; some of those canals are still in use today.

At the dawn of the 20th century, next to copper, cotton was king. J. G. Boswell's cotton empire would stretch from Northern California across to Arizona, displacing alfalfa and dairy farms. Tire companies like Dunlap, Firestone, and Goodyear relocated factories to Arizona to take advantage of the newly developed long-staple Egyptian cotton.

Major farming families of northeast Mesa—the Ellsworths, Gardiners, Habeebs, Ishikawas, McKellips, and Thayers—planted thousands of acres of alfalfa, canaigre, cantaloupes, corn, cotton, lettuce, sugar beets, and watermelons. They kept small herds of dairy cows, beef cattle, and sheep, and there were even some ostrich farms floating around the state.

But citrus crops were on the rise. As Jared Smith's outstanding book, *Making Water Flow Uphill: The History of Agriculture in Mesa, Arizona*, states, "In the late 1920s and early 1930s, a group of executives with the J. C. Penney Company decided to invest over $1 million in the development of a new citrus ranch northeast of Mesa." La Hermosa Vista Land and Cattle Company would plant some 1,200 acres of citrus, bordered approximately by what are now "McDowell Road to the north, Greenfield Road to the east, Brown Road to the south and Val Vista Drive to the west"—basically, the area surrounding Falcon Field.

When World War II began to sweep across Europe, what could a small town like Mesa, Arizona, do to help in the fight for freedom across the sea? In early 1941, residents were about to find out, for the city had been chosen as one of the six places in the United States to house a British training base.

The Germans were carrying on a continuous bombing campaign against the United Kingdom as part of a planned channel crossing and invasion. Combined with poor English weather conditions and a shortage of planes and fuel, it was difficult to train new pilots. In 1940, the British Royal Air Force (RAF) created the Empire Air Training Scheme, a massive air training program involving Australia, Canada, New Zealand, South Africa, and southern Rhodesia. Realizing that these efforts were not enough, the British struck a bargain with the United States to help train the enormous number of pilots needed to continue the war effort in Europe.

In the United States, Gen. Henry H. "Hap" Arnold, a World War I veteran, had taken his own steps toward this end, sending telegrams to eight private flying school operators and inviting them to meet him in Washington, D.C., to discuss the creation of civilian contract military training schools.

Meanwhile, former U.S. Navy pilot, World War I veteran, and Hollywood producer Leland Hayward was in the market for a new airplane. He met with John "Jack" Connelly, a pilot and aircraft salesman, at Chasen's Restaurant in Los Angeles. Hayward did not buy a plane, but the two men founded Southwest Airways and, with Hollywood money and a board of directors list that read like the Academy Award nomination ballots, built the Thunderbird Fields in Glendale and Scottsdale, Arizona, as well as civilian operations at Phoenix Sky Harbor.

In June 1941, Arizona senator Carl Hayden told the Associated Press that the Civil Aeronautics Authority had cleared the way for $350,000 to be used to build a British training base in Mesa and that the British Air Commission had agreed to finance 60 percent of the cost. British squadron leader Stuart Mills, wounded in the Battle of Norway, was sent to the United States to set up some of the fields, Arizona being his primary charge. He found the proposed Arizona field to be a lonely piece of desert located at the end of a narrow dirt road 7 miles northeast of the small town of Mesa. The field was a flat square mile of desert that the City of Mesa had purchased from agricultural giant Elias Habeeb, with citrus groves surrounding the area and Red Mountain a beautiful backdrop a few miles to the northeast.

The British and American flags were raised at ground-breaking ceremonies for the 720 acres of Mesa land at 10:30 a.m. on July 16, 1941, by Mesa mayor George N. Goodman and Arizona governor Sidney P. Osborn. Earlier that morning, they had attended the same for what would become Williams Field in south Mesa. Radio station KTAR broadcast both ceremonies.

Work began at the field immediately. In August, the building activity was stepped up when two carloads of building materials arrived. The *Mesa Tribune-Journal* reported on some of the work being done, "Under construction are eight barracks, each to provide housing for fifty cadets, a large building providing mess hall, kitchen, recreation room, hospital and other facilities, and four hangars."

The Mesa Chamber of Commerce set up a contest to give the field a name; 100 names were submitted. On July 31, 1941, the winner was selected. Falcon Field, the winning name, was submitted by E. B. Tucker, superintendent of streets for the city. A panel from Southwest Airways chose the winning name, which Tucker said symbolized "the famous English fighting spirit, and is the name of their renowned fighting and hunting bird. The insignia on the planes would be outstanding."

On September 14, 1941, the field officially opened. Even though the work on the field was far from over, the training had to begin. By September 26, there were already 144 men on the field. They ranged in age from 19 to 32 years old. This group, under the command of Flight Lt. E. C. Metcalf, had been training at Thunderbird I until Falcon was ready. Metcalf now became the director of training at Falcon Field. The RAF unit was commanded by squadron leader W. T. Holloway.

The first months of Falcon's operations were difficult on everyone. The plumbing problems turned those working on the field into milk drinkers. Classes were held against a backdrop of hammering, sawing, painting, and sawdust. The cadets sat on whatever was available in the barracks during class sessions while their beds were being painted. Outside, the airplanes taxied up and down the runway with the graders and steam rollers. Eventually the field was completed and all the bugs worked out . . . except for the crickets, scorpions, and rattlesnakes that would regularly invade the property.

Every five weeks, a new group of cadets would arrive, some Americans, some Canadians, mostly British. With their country being bombed constantly, with wartime rationing and shortages, as Jim Dawson states in his extremely detailed book, *The RAF in Arizona: Falcon Field, 1941–1945*, "For the cadets from Great Britain, Falcon was a brief respite from the war, a magical wonderland with fresh oranges, beautiful girls, and 600hp airplanes that literally screamed over the desert sand. And then there were the 200 automobiles that lined up at the main gate each weekend to take the cadets to private homes for fellowship and home-cooked meals."

Part of the magic came from the Hollywood connection. Stars like Hoagy Carmichael, Henry Fonda, Jimmy Stewart, and Darryl Zanuck were constantly coming and going from Falcon. In 1942, Fox made a movie at Thunderbird I and Falcon Field called *Thunder Birds*, starring Gene Tierney, Preston Foster, John Sutton, Reginald Denny, and Jack Holt. British and Chinese cadets were used as extras, but because they were active-duty military personnel, the studio could not pay them for their work. So as a thank-you, Fox built a swimming pool in the center of the yard between the barracks. (It was demolished in 2004.)

With the announcement of the Course 25 graduation on August 25, 1945, Falcon Field officials also announced that the field would be closing on September 11, 1945, having graduated over 1,500 cadets since its opening. Course 25 cadets were honored with a dinner dance at the Westward Ho Hotel, and within a week, everyone was gone but the administrative officer and the accountant. Thunderbird II had closed in October 1944, and Thunderbird I was closed in June 1945. The Japanese surrendered August 14, 1945, and the war was over.

The City of Mesa took back possession of the field for $1. For the next decade or so, Mesa city officials like Virgil Crismon, Rial Randall, and Leonard Sale actively sought tenants for the airfield. The Mesa Airport Authority was incorporated in 1951.

Jim and Vera Dingman opened Sunshine Acres Children's Home just up the road from Falcon in 1954, but nothing developed at Falcon Field until 1957, when the City of Mesa leased the property out to various Talley defense subsidiaries such as Astro Rocket, Inc., and Rocket Power, Inc. Construction of test facilities on the airport property was completed in September of that year. The control tower and an available aircraft hangar became office space and workspace, respectively. Activities involving the small number of aircraft using the airfield were limited to another nearby hangar. Testing of Talco's larger devices was immediately started in Mesa, and by the end of 1957, the drafting and engineering activities began relocating to the Mesa Division.

In the early 1960s, men like Pete Miller, Gene Packard, Abe Sellards, and Floyd Stilwell (who cranked Stearman engines for the British at Falcon when he was in high school) began setting up shop at Falcon Field with companies like Aircraft Specialties, Inc., and Globe Air. Packard and Stilwell are still in business, with Air Response, Inc., and Marsh Aviation, respectively. Other early companies, like Superstition Air Services (SAS), live on through acquisition by Falcon Executive Aircraft, Inc., run by Paul Lessaongang, who started out washing planes for SAS. Yet other companies, like Nichols Flying Service, Miller Aircraft, and Petella-Wischler Crop Dusting Service, are long gone.

The decades that followed would bring in many more businesses. J&J Materials opened on the southeast corner of the Falcon Field property. The Boeing Company facility just across McDowell Road was originally built as a Hughes Helicopter factory. Residential acreage grew as well. Alta Mea, a master-planned community of over 2,500 homes, sprang up on Higley, just south of the airport and the Apache Wells community across Higley to the east.

In the early 21st century, another boom came, with over 200,000 square feet of commercial and office space, including the Longbow Golf Club across the northeast corner from the airport and several business parks surrounding. The Falcon Field Business District now comprises some 7,000 acres surrounding the airport and over 18,000 employees. Major corporations include Alliant Techsystems (ATK), the Boeing Company, Lockheed-Martin, Marsh Aviation, MD Helicopters, Inc., Nammo Talley, Semflex, SolFocus, Special Devices, Inc., Timken, Trans-Matic, and Waxie Sanitary Supply.

But the orange groves survive . . . for now.

As Lori P. Roberts states in her 2002 dissertation on Falcon Field, "British cadets trained at Falcon Field had fond memories of their stay in Arizona. Many cadets, instructors or staff of Falcon chose to remain or eventually return to the Valley after training ended." Some of them included Ken and Dorothy Beeby, Norman Dibble, Laurie and Molly Turner, and Joe and Ruth Wischler.

Dawson's book states it best, "Thirty-four years after the war ended, the 'boys' of Falcon formed an association [the Falcon Field Association (FFA)] and held . . . reunions, not because they served in the same combat squadrons, but because they learned to fly at the same place, a place called Falcon Field." What a testament that is, that this lonely patch of airstrip in the desert, founded at the height of the world's darkest days, still can bring people together, bring money into Mesa's economy, teach younger generations, and tug at the heartstrings of those who understand war and what it meant.

The importance of Falcon Field is multifaceted. Its history proves that ordinary people, in ordinary places, working together, could make a difference in the outcome of a world war. It proved that people sharing their lives with people of another culture could have a great impact on their future and ours. The field not only is an important part of Mesa's history, but American and world history as well.

At the time of this writing, as time edges into the 21st century, more and more members of the Greatest Generation pass away, and as those left, both in the FFA and the Daughters of the British Empire (DBE), with whom the FFA held remembrance ceremonies at the Mesa Cemetery for decades, are hitting their late 80s and early 90s, there are plans to close down the FFA and the future of the remembrance ceremony future is imperiled.

It is up to Mesans, Arizonans, Americans, and members of the human race to preserve Falcon Field not only as an asset for those who love to fly, but also preserve it as a living memorial to the cadets, instructors, field staff, Mesa citizens, and citizens of the surrounding area whose work helped keep freedom ringing throughout the world in its most difficult hours. And it is also a fitting memorial to those who died, whether training at the field or in battle to preserve freedom, through struggles to the stars—*per ardua ad astra.*

—Daryl F. Mallett and Connie Gullatt-Whiteman

One

Earliest Inhabitants

The Hohokam ("Those Who Have Gone" or "The Departed Ones") were one of four major prehistoric peoples from the American Southwest. They lived in an area that stretched from approximately Flagstaff, Arizona, to the Mexican border, with the center being roughly at the middle Gila River and lower Salt River area, which includes Mesa.

Between the 7th and 14th centuries, they built and maintained an extensive network of irrigation canals for their agricultural needs, nearly 125 miles worth, which irrigated some 100,000 acres of land. For the time period, the canal system could have rivaled similar systems in the Middle East. Archaeologists have discovered they grew agave, beans, cotton, maize, squash, and tobacco in addition to harvesting wild plants. Some of the canals were rejuvenated by the first settlers in the area and are still in use to this day.

Besides the canal system, their architecture featured sunken ball courts and pyramidal mounds, leading scientists to surmise that they migrated north into the Arizona area around 300 BC. Examples of their buildings survive in locations like Casa Grande, Mesa, Phoenix, Santan, and Tempe, Arizona.

They were creative in their artwork, known for their intricate coiled pottery designs, stone tools, woven cotton textiles, petroglyphs, anthropomorphic and zoomorphic figurines, and shell work, enjoying good trade relations with their Anasazi, Mogollon, and Patayan neighbors, as well as groups farther south, as evidenced by remains of parrots and copper bells.

Their fate is unknown, but they disappeared sometime between 1450 AD and the arrival of the Spanish conquistadores. It is possible that the Hohokam may be the ancestors of the Akimel Au-Authm ("River People"/Pima), Hia C-ed O'odham ("Sand Dune People"/Sand Pimas or Sand Papagos), Tohono O'odham ("Desert People"/Papago), and Xalychidom Piipaash ("People Who Live Toward the Water"/Maricopa) nations, as well as several extinct tribes, such as the Sobaipuri.

The Hohokam ("Those Who Have Gone") were one of the four primary peoples of the Southwestern United States, flourishing from about 1 to 1450 AD. They may be the ancestors of the Sto'am

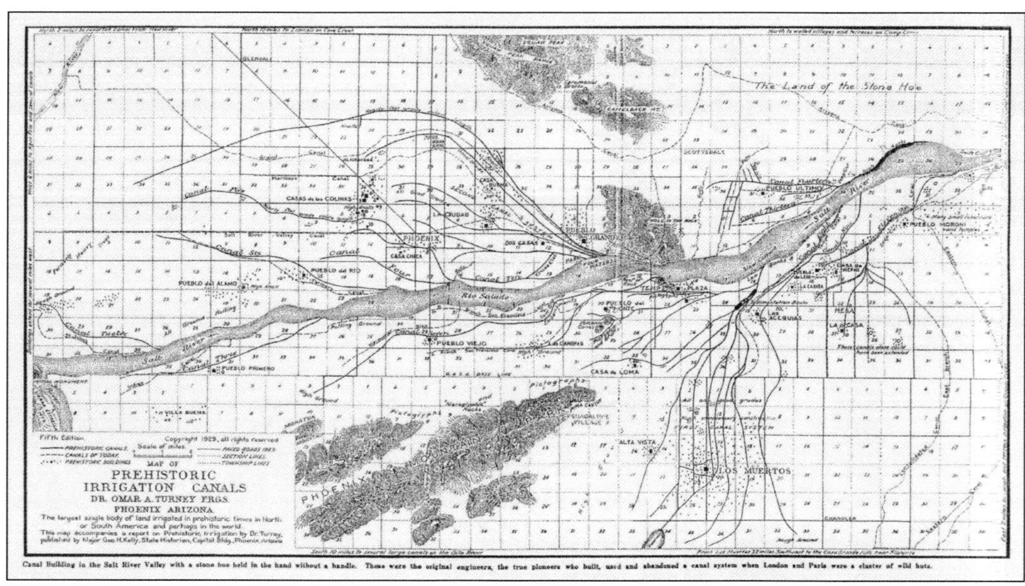

A network of simple dirt canals and weirs was built by the Hohokam throughout the Southwestern United States that rivaled those used in Egypt and China. (Courtesy of SRP.)

O'odham ("Coyote People"), Akimel O'odham, Tohono O'odham, Sobaipuri, and Pima-Maricopa nations. (Photograph by author, artwork courtesy of Mesa Historical Museum.)

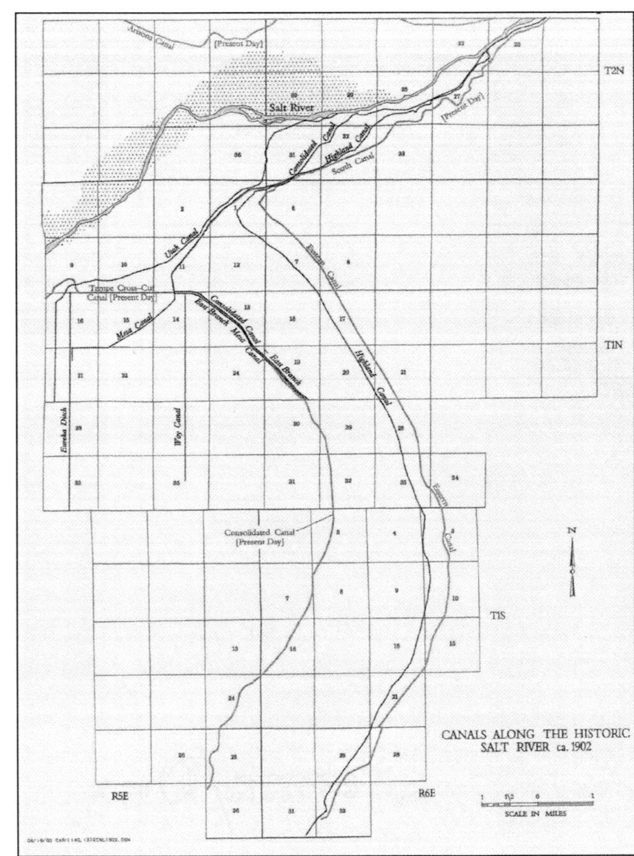

Between the 7th and 14th centuries, they built an extensive irrigation system to serve their crops of beans, cotton, maize, squash, and tobacco. Various maps exist, most of which are similar to each other but not quite exact matches. (Courtesy of SRP.)

The Utah Ditch and the Highland Ditch in Mesa, Arizona, are two of many dirt canals that were built by the Hohokam throughout the Southwestern United States. (Both courtesy of SRP.)

The Utah Ditch and the Highland Ditch were both built by the Hohokam and improved upon by the Lehi settlers. Some sections are still in use today. (Both courtesy of SRP.)

Casa Grande was a major structure built during the Hohokam Classic Period (1100–1450 AD). The 3,000-ton caliche structure is believed to have been built during the 1300s. The above photograph, taken by Cosmos Mindeleff, shows the structure in 1890. Wind and rain were eroding the structure, so Pres. Benjamin Harrison created the Casa Grande Ruin Reservation to preserve the one-of-a-kind structure. In 1918, Pres. Woodrow Wilson renamed the park the Casa Grande National Monument. A roof, seen below, was built over the structure in 1903, followed by several others. The current roof was finished on December 12, 1932. The site is still utilized by local Native American tribes for special ceremonies. (Both courtesy of National Parks Service, U.S. Department of the Interior.)

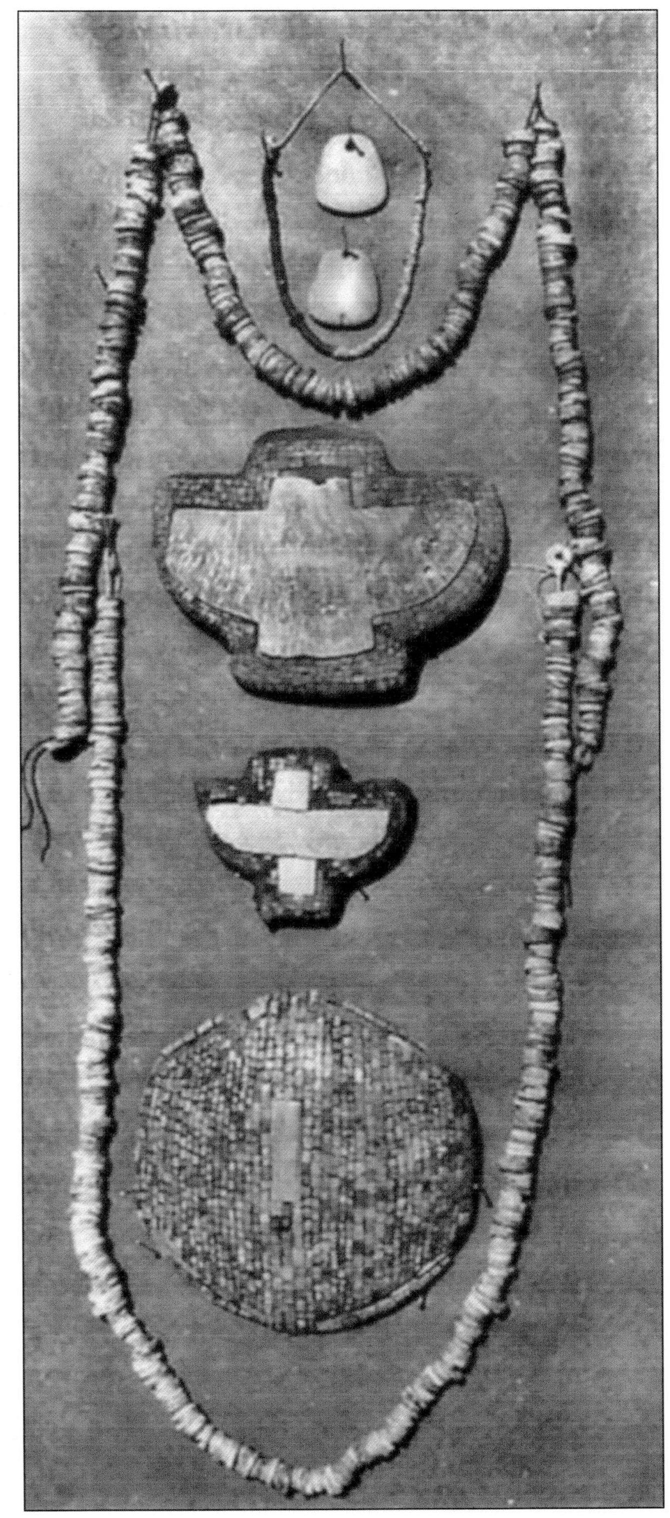

The Hohokam are credited with being the first culture to master acid etching. Artisans also produced jewelry from shell, stone, and bone. These turquoise mosaics were discovered in 1925 at the Casa Grande Ruins National Monument in Arizona. (Courtesy of National Parks Service, U.S. Department of the Interior.)

The Hohokam created a wide range of rock art, also known as petroglyphs or pictographs, throughout the Arizona area, including the one seen below that may be the only known record of a supernova witnessed in 1006 AD. (Both photographs by Mark Goldstein.)

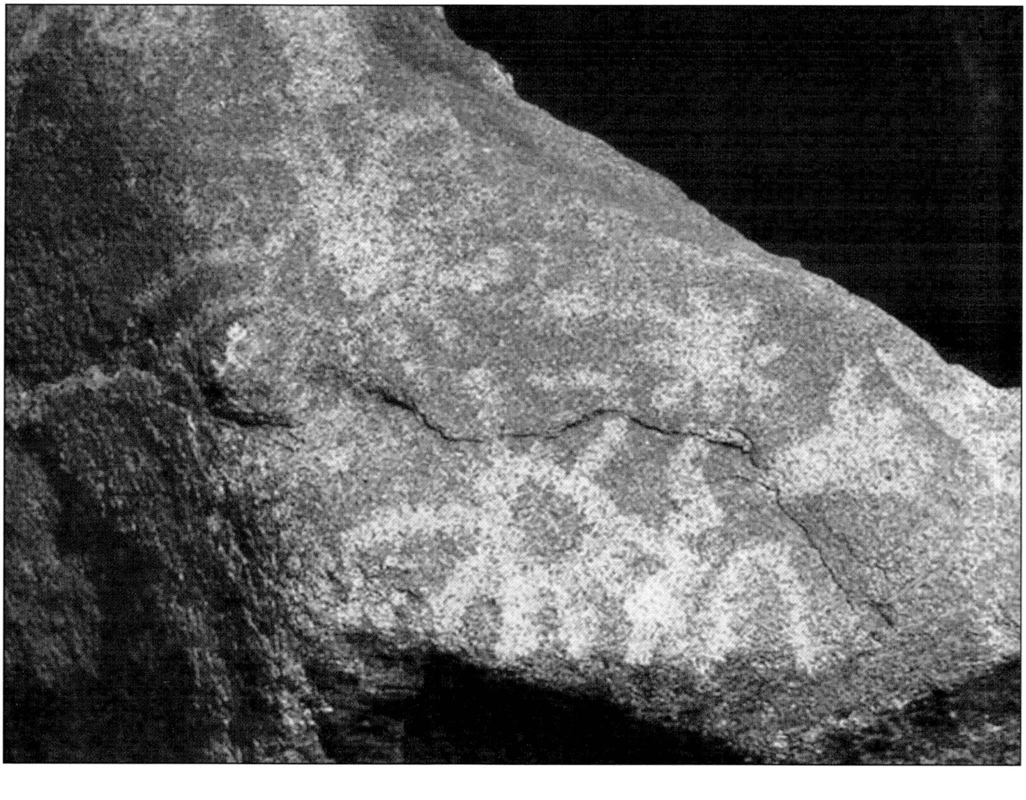

The Salt River Pima-Maricopa Indian Community, established in 1879, is located in an urbanized area bordered by Scottsdale, Mesa, and Tempe, Arizona. These two nations, the Pima (or Akimel Au-Authm/"River People") and the Maricopa (or Xalychidom Piipaash/"People Who Live Toward the Water"), are probable descendants of the Hohokam. (Courtesy of Federal Highway Administration, U.S. Department of Transportation.)

The Salt River Pima-Maricopa Indian Community is a vibrant community involved in various economic development enterprises, such as agriculture, casinos, golf courses, museums, landfills, construction materials, gas, other natural resources, and more. (Photograph by author.)

Talking Stick Resort—complete with a 497 deluxe hotel room/15 luxury suite hotel, retail outlets, spa amenities, business car rental companies, a conference center, and a 240,000-square-foot casino—was opened at the Talking Stick Golf Club site in 2010. (Photograph by Adrian Teo.)

Mount McDowell, commonly known as "Red Mountain," is one of the most prominent geological features on Salt River Pima-Maricopa Indian Community land. Created by the erosion of highlands

Designers Bill Coore and Ben Crenshaw created the Talking Stick Golf Club. Two unique courses offer many options to the level of the golfer's playing skill. The Talking Stick golf courses are located on and owned by the Salt River Pima-Maricopa Indian Community. (Courtesy of Casino Arizona and Talking Stick Golf Club.)

pushed up 30 million years ago, the mountain is 2,830 feet high. (Photograph by author.)

Mount McDowell is named for Gen. Irvin McDowell (1818–1885). A graduate of West Point in 1838, the Ohio-born McDowell served in the Mexican-American War under the flag of Gen. John Ellis Wool (1784–1869). During the Civil War, he was defeated at the First Battle of Bull Run. McDowell worked with Gen. John Charles Frémont (1813–1890), who also has many features and buildings named for him in Mesa. (Courtesy of U.S. National Archives and Records Administration.)

Two

New Settlers

In 1877, Daniel Webster Jones (1830–1915) led a group of Mormon settlers from Utah and Idaho to the banks of the Salt River, where they founded the settlement of Lehi. They befriended the native people and resurrected some of the Hohokam canals for use in their agricultural pursuits.

They were quickly followed by the First Mesa Company, led by Charles Crismon Sr. (1805–1890), Francis Martin Pomeroy (1822–1882), Charles Innes Robson I (1837–1894), and George W. Sirrine (1818–1902), who moved up the mesa to what is now downtown Mesa. The Second Mesa Company, led by Charles Carrol "Carl" Dana (1832–1901), John Anderson Hibbert (1822–1903), John Taylor LeSueur (1852–1945), and Hyrum Smith Phelps (1846–1926), arrived less than a year later. These families moved up the mesa from Lehi and founded what is now the city of Mesa in 1878. Two years later, another group, led by Chancey Foster Rogers (1829–1899), Henry M. Standage (1818–1899), and Charles Orrin Pew (1860–1937), came and founded the Stringtown area of Mesa.

Dr. A. J. Chandler (1859–1950), who later founded the city bearing his name south of Mesa, was instrumental in the growth of the city. He enlarged the Mesa Canal with heavy machinery, built the first office complex in the city on the northwest corner of Main and Macdonald Streets, utilized the first evaporative air cooling system in Arizona, and started an electric power plant. The City of Mesa purchased the utility company from Chandler in 1917, becoming one of the few cities in Arizona to own its own utilities.

Hispanics were already in the area before 1890, including the Aros, Candelaria, Castro, Garcia, and Rivera families. Ramon Mendoza Sr. was the first Hispanic police officer in Mesa; his son would become the first Hispanic police chief. The first black family, the McPhersons, arrived in 1905. Dr. James Livingston, a black veterinarian, arrived before 1910; other blacks who arrived before 1920 were the Ferguson, Hall, Kemp, McKelvy, and Moore families. Chinese families, such as the Homs, Lees, and Yees, and Japanese families, such as the Horibas, Ikedas, Nishidas, Okazakis, and Suginos, also began arriving about 1910. Willie Wong, mayor of Mesa (1992–1996) and the first Asian mayor of a major city; Barry Wong, former Arizona Corporation Commissioner and state representative; and Zedo Ishikawa, former Mesa High School football star, are from these founding families, and many of them still live and work in Arizona.

The First Mesa Company, comprised of 85 members, left Utah and Idaho in September 1877. The company leaders were Charles Crismon Sr., Francis Martin Pomeroy, Charles Innes Robson I, and George W. Sirrine. They took a different route from the Lehi Company, crossing the Colorado River at Lee's Ferry, where there is a steep cliff across the river. The leaders of the Mesa Company reached Utahville, as Lehi or Jonesville was then called, in January 1878; the rest of the company came in February. They decided to move up to the mesa and began marking off land and clearing the original Hohokam canals; water entered the canals in April. On July 17, 1878, Theodore Charles Sirrine went to Florence, Arizona, to register Section 22, now called the Town Center: the square mile from Mesa Drive to Country Club Drive and University Drive to Broadway Road. (Courtesy of Orson Pratt Brown Family Organization.)

Daniel Webster Jones (1830–1915), who was the grandfather of actress Fay Wray, led the expedition that left St. George, Utah, in March 1877 to settle the Mesa, Arizona, area. Originally called Jonesville, the settlement was eventually renamed Fort Utah, and then Lehi in 1883, which was later incorporated into Mesa. (Courtesy of Orson Pratt Brown Family Organization.)

Alexander Findlay MacDonald (1825–1903) was born in Scotland. After meeting Mormon missionaries in 1846, he moved to Canada, then the United States and Mexico. He served as the Maricopa Stake of Zion's first president and Mesa's first mayor before moving to Mexico to settle a Mormon colony in Colonia Juarez. (Courtesy of Orson Pratt Brown Family Organization.)

The Mormon Temple in Mesa was the seventh one built, from reinforced concrete and 130 tons of steel. The ground was broken on April 25, 1922, and it was dedicated for use in October 1927. The 114,000-square-foot facility was the object of many firsts: the first temple built in Arizona, the first to offer services in a language other than English (Spanish, in 1945), the first to reopen to the public for an open house prior to a rededication, and the first built with no spires or towers. It served members of the Church of Jesus Christ of Latter-day Saints throughout the state of Arizona, including those who lived near Falcon Field. (Courtesy of Molly Turner.)

Adobe is a natural building material made from sand, clay, and water, with fibrous or organic materials, such as sticks, straw, or dung, shaped into bricks using frames and dried in the sun. Some of the oldest extant buildings in the world are made from adobe, and it was a prevalent building style in the Southwestern United States when the Mormon settlers arrived in Arizona in the 1870s. This building, located in Lehi, Arizona, would have been a common sight. (Courtesy of Orson Pratt Brown Family Organization.)

The settlers in Lehi built a brickyard and began to construct houses. With a dearth of trees in the area, lumber still had to be imported via horse-and-buggy until the railroad arrived in Mesa in 1895. Several early brick buildings still exist in Mesa, including the Joel E. Sirrine House and Biggs home (the latter of which was the first permanent separate house in Lehi, originally built of adobe but replaced by brick in the 1890s) and the Old Lehi School, where the Mesa Historical Museum is now located. (Courtesy of Mesa Public Library.)

The first store in Mesa was the Biggs General Merchandise Store, built around 1880 by Thomas Biggs (died 1886). It burned down, but this was their second store, built in about 1892. Later the Lehi Post Office was located here for several years. The store is still standing and has been the home of a carpenter shop, among other things, and is currently a community building located across the street from the original auditorium of the Lehi School, now the Mesa Historical Museum. (Courtesy of Mesa Public Library.)

Downtown Mesa was a far cry from Falcon Field in the 1940s, with little traffic moving between the city and the field. Royal Air Force cadet Ken Beeby, who trained at Falcon, related a story of walking "seven or eight miles from the airbase to downtown Mesa" or hitching a ride when they were available. (Courtesy of Molly Turner.)

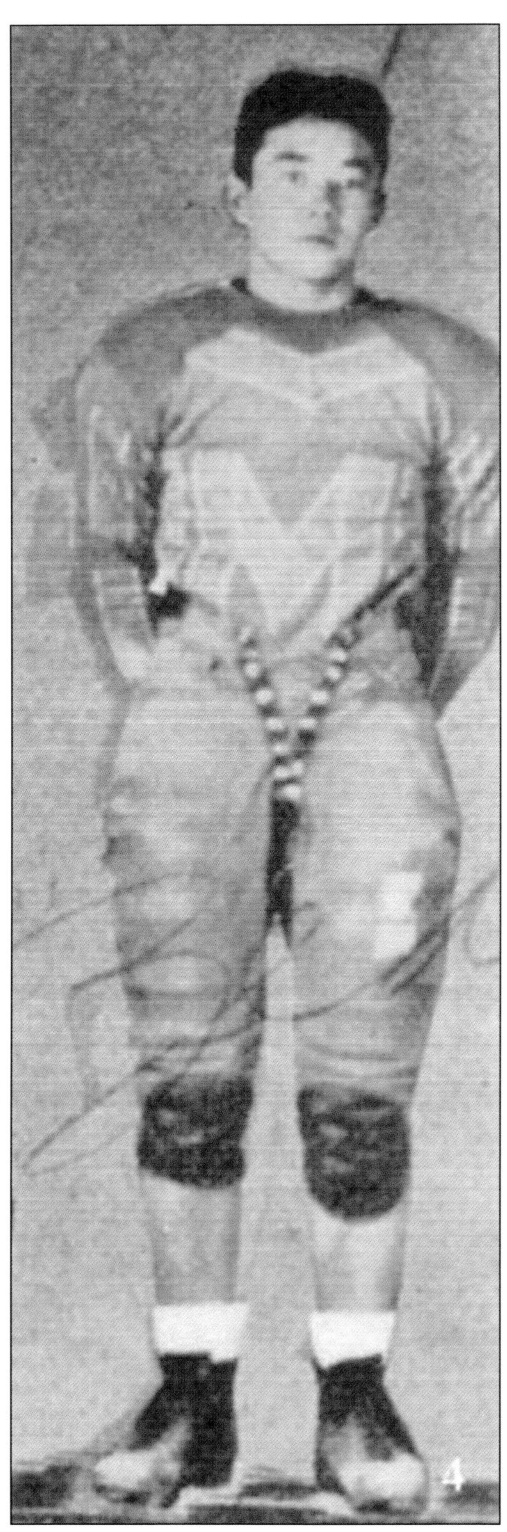

Zedo Ishikawa (1915–1932) was a member of one of Arizona's first Japanese families. Raised in the Lehi District of Mesa, he was active in Boy Scouts and was a star football player his senior year at Mesa High School. He was killed in a gun accident the night before opening day of the football season in 1932, and his final words—"Tell coach to go ahead and play the game tomorrow. Tell the boys to carry on"—inspired the school's motto, "Carry On." An elementary school was named in his honor in Mesa in 1987. Other families included the Ikedas, Motoyoshis, and Okazakis. (Courtesy of Mesa Public Schools, City of Mesa.)

Three

Agricultural Community

Jared Smith's in-depth book, *Making Water Flow Uphill: The History of Agriculture in Mesa*, states:

> The story of agriculture in Mesa is in many ways the history of the town itself. Farming was at the heart of the community from its very beginning, and remained so until the early 1970s. Lehi, Mesa's sister community to the north, is where this story begins. Settled by a hearty group of Latter-Day Saint colonists in 1877, Lehi grew into a small, independent farming community after a difficult beginning. While the story of Mesa began in 1877, the deepest roots of agriculture in the region go back many centuries to the Hohokam, who carved untold hundreds of miles of canals throughout the region, including the one that would be revamped as the Mesa Canal in 1878.
>
> After hard beginnings, the communities of Mesa and Lehi developed thriving agricultural economies that were preeminent, both in the Salt River Valley and throughout most of the Southwestern U.S. These towns often rivaled and even surpassed the agricultural output of their neighbors, Phoenix and Glendale, with crops like alfalfa, citrus, cotton and grapes. Mesa farmers were also innovative and willing to gamble on the success of new crops like canaigre, sugar beets, cantaloupes and long-staple cotton. And no story of local agriculture would be complete without telling of the Salt River Project and the struggle to build massive water storage reservoirs, especially Roosevelt Dam.
>
> There were ups-and-downs, from the heady days of the cotton boom during World War I, to the massive Cotton Bust that followed—an event that local residents called the worst depression the region ever suffered. In the late 1920s/early 1930s, the citrus industry boomed in Mesa and Lehi, and the industry managed to weather the Great Depression. World War II brought another boom to the area, followed by a revolution in mechanization, when tractors finally replaced horse's once-and-for-all on local farms. From the beginning, a dizzying array of crops and livestock were raised in Mesa. Even now, long after the sun has set on the heyday of local agriculture, names like Dobson Ranch and McKellips Road are familiar to many residents as synonymous with the glory days of Mesa and its farming heritage. Today, evidence of Mesa and Lehi's former agricultural empire appears only in small patches scattered here and there in Mesa, squeezed in between malls, massive housing developments, and freeways.

These empty fields are what east Mesa looked like before Elias Habeeb, Chauncey H. McKellips, Kurataro Ishikawa, and other citrus pioneers and farmers began planting crops in the area. Jim Beasley (in the large white hat) oversees the planting of the first orange groves on the McKellips Ranch. (Photograph by Joel Clair Franks, courtesy of Joan Franks Gannon.)

Tiny orange trees dot the landscape as Joel Clair Franks (on the right), McKellips's foreman, takes a drive through the groves to inspect the crops. (Courtesy of Joan Franks Gannon.)

A large system of canals was already in place, dating back to the Hohokam Indians, hundreds of years before white settlers arrived in Mesa. The canals were expanded by the Lehi Company settlers. Workers constructed large pumps to move the water from the canals into the irrigation system in the fields. (Photograph by Joel Clair Franks, courtesy of Joan Franks Gannon.)

Canals had to be continuously dredged to keep from being blocked by debris. This giant dredge was available to clean them out. (Photograph by Joel Clair Franks, courtesy of Joan Franks Gannon.)

Extension canals had to be built to move water from the large canal system into the irrigation system feeding the fields. Ernie Jones (center) oversees the construction of the feeder canals. (Photograph by Joel Clair Franks, courtesy of Joan Franks Gannon.)

Even after the trees were planted, the feeder canals were built, and the pumps were working, there was still a lot of work to do. From left to right, Joel Clair Franks, Buster Woodard, Pinto the dog, and Kirby Leffel work on grading the roads in and out of the groves. (Courtesy of Joan Franks Gannon.)

Kirby Leffel (left), Jim Beasley (center) and Joel Clair Franks are seen here with the heavy equipment, ready to go out and grade roads. (Courtesy of Joan Franks Gannon.)

Buster (back) and Kirby Leffel grade the orchard roads with heavy equipment. (Photograph by Joel Clair Franks, courtesy of Joan Franks Gannon.)

Taking care of the groves required a lot of work. R. Ruiz (left) and Jim Beasley spray down the trees with fertilizer, water, and pesticides. (Photograph by Joel Clair Franks, courtesy of Joan Franks Gannon.)

Joel Clair Franks was the foreman for C. H. McKellips, overseeing everything from citrus to cotton and sheep to alfalfa, and he seemed to be everywhere at once. He spent 25 years working for McKellips and another five for the new owners. He then moved out to Bullhead City to work with McKellips again, this time focusing on cotton. (Courtesy of Joan Franks Gannon.)

On January 30, 1937, Mesa experienced its largest ever snowfall, with a record 3 inches falling. The temperature plummeted to a record low of 21 degrees Fahrenheit. The citrus crops in Mesa were devastated. Chauncey McKellips, founder of McKellips Mutual Citrus Growers, Inc., came out to examine the damage to his orange crops, which still stand along the western and southwestern outskirts of Falcon Field. (Photograph by Joel Clair Franks, courtesy of Joan Franks Gannon.)

Fortunately the trees survived the snowfall. George Webb strolls through the groves, taking a break from picking oranges. (Photograph by Joel Clair Franks, courtesy of Joan Franks Gannon.)

In the 1940s, old school met regularly with new technology. Horse-drawn wagons and motorized trucks side by side hauling oranges out of the groves would not have been an uncommon sight. (Photograph by Joel Clair Franks, courtesy of Joan Franks Gannon.)

Crop dusting was effective against thrips and mites but was limited for several reasons, such as the need for several applications to obtain suitable control and the repetition of applications affected by rainfall and wind. (Photograph by Joel Clair Franks, courtesy of Joan Franks Gannon.)

McKellips and Habeeb were two of the biggest names in citrus farming in northeast Mesa in the 1940s and 1950s. Falcon Field sits on land purchased from the Habeeb family. McKellips sold his groves in 1955 to Hermosa Vista. (Both photographs by author, artwork from the Mesa Historical Museum.)

The Mesa Citrus Growers Association is located on Broadway Road at Country Club Drive in Mesa. Founded in 1935, the facility could pack some 800,000 boxes of fruit a year. Many northeast Mesa growers participated in its development and operations. It is still packing approximately 500,000 boxes of fruit per year (Courtesy of Rex Griswold.)

Alfalfa and cotton were some of the main crops grown in northeast Mesa. (Photograph by Joel Clair Franks, courtesy of Joan Franks Gannon.)

According to Jared Smith's book *Making Water Flow Uphill: The History of Agriculture in Mesa, Arizona*, cotton was a staple crop, "Tens of thousands of acres of land around Mesa were covered with crops, ranging from alfalfa, cotton, and corn, to unusual and often short lived crops like canaigre [a member of the buckwheat family, similar to rhubarb] and sugar beets. . . . In the late 1800s, there had even been a thriving wine-making industry, supported by hundreds of acres of vineyards." Joan (left) and Joyce Franks (right), daughters-in-law of Joel Clair Franks, worked on the cotton harvest at the McKellips Ranch. (Photograph by Joel Clair Franks, courtesy of Joan Franks Gannon.)

Melons were also a large crop in Mesa, with watermelons long being a staple. About 1900, a new melon arrived—the Rocky Ford sugar melons, also known as cantaloupes, which took the state by storm. (Courtesy of SRP.)

Farmers also raised sheep and "drove" them to market, sometimes using their cars. Jared Smith's book continues, "In addition to beef cattle, milk cows, sheep, and most of the other animals associated with farms, ostriches once roamed the countryside on large ranches through the Salt River Valley." Bees were also raised in large apiaries. According to Joan Franks Gannon, the Hemphill family had a chicken farm on Val Vista Road, between McDowell and McKellips Roads. (Courtesy of SRP.)

This red-brick house on McKellips Road, just west of Greenfield, was paid for by Chauncey McKellips and given as a gift to the Franks family because Mae McKellips wanted Joan Franks, Joel's only daughter among seven siblings, to have her own bedroom and bathroom. The house still stands today, and the family living in it works at the orange stand next door. Jack Gannon and Joan Franks had their wedding reception on the front lawn. (Photograph by Joel Clair Franks, courtesy of Joan Franks Gannon.)

Horses were still in just as much use as cars on the ranch. Here two horses are tied up at the post behind the Frankses' house. (Photograph by Joel Clair Franks, courtesy of Joan Franks Gannon.)

Dan and Joan Franks, seen here on a bicycle in 1941, grew up in the house at McKellips Road and Lindsay Road and used to pedal past Falcon Field regularly. (Photograph by Joel Clair Franks, courtesy of Joan Franks Gannon.)

Four

Founding Falcon Field

U.S. general Henry H. "Hap" Arnold knew the United States would require additional air training bases if it were to enter World War II. Congress authorized one additional training base. Disappointed with the results, Arnold invited eight civilian flight operators to discuss his idea in Washington, D.C.

Meanwhile, aircraft salesman and former test pilot John H. "Jack" Connelly and famed Hollywood producer and former U.S. Navy pilot Leland Hayward met at Chasen's Restaurant in Los Angeles. The two men formed Southwest Airways, intended for training pilots. Hayward secured money from producers William Goetz and Darryl Zanuck, talent agent Bert Allenberg, studio executive Ben Goetz, composer Hoagy Carmichael, Broadway producer Gilbert Miller, director Mervyn LeRoy, photographer John Swope, and actors Henry Fonda, Cary Grant, Dorothy McGuire, Ginger Rogers, and Jimmy Stewart.

RAF squadron leader Stuart Mills was the first one scouting sites. The *AAHS Journal* relates, "On his arrival at Phoenix Sky Harbor Airport, he was met by Jack Connelly, Leland Hayward and Al Storrs (later to be director of training at Falcon Field). They immediately headed out for the proposed location of the field."

Originally slated to be Thunderbird Field III (No. 1 was opened in Glendale, Arizona; No. 2 in Scottsdale, Arizona), the name was nixed by RAF officials, who opted instead for Falcon Field since, as Sgt. Ken Beeby, who trained at Falcon, said, "The thunderbird sounded like a good, strong animal, but it wasn't British. It's distinctly American."

The British and American flags were raised at ground-breaking ceremonies for the 720 acres of Mesa land at 10:30 a.m. on July 16, 1941, by Mesa mayor George N. Goodman and Arizona governor Sidney P. Osborn. Work began at the field immediately. In August, the building activity was stepped up when two carloads of building materials arrived. The *Mesa Tribune-Journal* reported on some of the work being done, "Under construction are eight barracks, each to provide housing for fifty cadets, a large building providing mess hall, kitchen, recreation room, hospital and other facilities, and four hangars."

The first cadets arrived in September 1941.

Gen. Henry H. "Hap" Arnold conceived the idea to train Allied pilots in the United States before the it entered World War II. Acting on his own initiative, he sent telegrams to eight private flying school operators. As a result, airfields began to open across the country. (Courtesy of U.S. Department of Defense.)

Hollywood producer and World War I U.S. Navy pilot Leland Hayward (1902–1971) was trying to buy an airplane in the late 1930s. He agreed to meet with John Howard "Jack" Connelly, a pilot and aircraft salesman. Hayward was also a member of the board of directors for Transcontinental and Western Airlines (TWA). (Photograph by John Florea, courtesy of Gwen Florea.)

Pilot and aircraft salesman John Howard "Jack" Connelly (1900–1971) had the good fortune to meet with Hollywood producer Leland Hayward, who was in the market for an airplane. (Courtesy of Pima Air and Space Museum.)

This may be the very booth at Chasen's Restaurant in Los Angeles where Leland Hayward and John Howard "Jack" Connelly met to discuss the former's purchase of an airplane. Hayward did not buy a plane, but the meeting led to the formation of Southwest Airways, the Thunderbird Fields, and Falcon Field in Arizona. (Courtesy of www.latimemachines.com.)

Southwest Airways was founded with financing from friends and colleagues of Leland Hayward. Film, television, and theater types included Bert Allenberg, Hoagy Carmichael, Henry Fonda, Ben Goetz, William Goetz, Cary Grant, Floyd L. Hendrickson, Mervyn LeRoy, Dorothy McGuire, Gilbert Miller, Daniel T. O'Shea, James G. Ray, Walter Roche, Ginger Rogers, Harry E. Sokolov, Jimmy Stewart, John Swope, and Darryl F. Zanuck, among many others. Connelly would be president and CEO; Hayward would be director of operations, with John Swope as secretary/treasurer. The company has followed the standard long and torturous road of air carriers and is now part of Delta Airlines. (Courtesy of Ruth Wischler and Carolyn Wischler McDaniel.)

Actor Jimmy Stewart was one of the financiers of Southwest Airways. He also had a notable military career, achieving the rank of brigadier general in the U.S. Air Force Reserves. He occasionally attended the memorial ceremony at Mesa City Cemetery. (Courtesy of U.S. Department of Defense.)

Thunderbird Field I was the first of the Southwest Airways training schools in Arizona, used for contract primary flight training of Allied pilots in World War II. Founded in 1940, it was designed in the shape of a thunderbird, which could be seen from the air. After the war, the property was sold as surplus. The Thunderbird Graduate School of Management (founded in 1946 by Lt. Gen. Barton K. Yount, retired commander of the U.S. Army Air Forces Training Command, as the American Institute of Foreign Trade) is now located on the site. (Photograph by Peter Stackpole, courtesy of Anne Stackpole.)

Chinese and American pilots pose together for a publicity photograph at Thunderbird Field I. Pilots from Chang Kai-Shek's army trained in Glendale. British RAF pilots trained in Mesa at Falcon Field. Pilots from Russia, South American countries, and nearly 30 Allied nations trained in Arizona throughout the war. (Photograph by Peter Stackpole, courtesy of Anne Stackpole.)

Soldiers and airmen were always up for entertainment. Because of the prominent Hollywood icons involved in the founding of the Arizona training bases, cadets were often treated to the presence of stars. The Earl Carroll Theatre, above, was a favorite hangout for the likes of Darryl F. Zanuck and Walter Wanger, and the cadets were always welcome to come and dance with the stars, as Leading Aircraftman Tom Austin (Course 5) does below. (Above, photograph by Eric Geoffrey Hutchin, courtesy of Catherine Hutchin Harris; below, courtesy of Tom Austin.)

Course 11 cadets, from left to right, LAC Thomas Watt "Jock" Briggs (KIA February 15, 1944), Sgt. Ken Beeby, Sgt. Arthur Meakin "Bottles" Armin (KIA May 23, 1944), Sgt. Norman I. Ballance, and an unidentified corporal pose with actress Alice Faye (1915–1998) at Hollywood Studios. (Courtesy of Ken Beeby.)

Darryl F. Zanuck was one of the writers of *Thunder Birds* (1942) and utilized Falcon Field and the Thunderbird Fields in Arizona for many of the locations. British and Chinese cadets served as extras in the film, and many of them were treated with access to the 20th Century Fox Studios. (Photograph by Eric Geoffrey Hutchin, courtesy of Catherine Hutchin Harris.)

The beautiful Gene Tierney starred in *Thunder Birds* and was photographed by everyone on the base who owned or could borrow a camera. She and her husband, Oleg Cassini, always welcomed the cadets at their Hollywood home for pool parties and visits. (Courtesy of Jim Dawson.)

Actors from the movie, like Reginald Denny (third from right), were more than happy to meet and pose with the cadets during the filming of *Thunder Birds* at Falcon Field. (Courtesy of Ruth Wischler and Carolyn Wischler McDaniel.)

Preston Foster, Reginald Denny, and Jack Holt spent many hours at Falcon Field shooting scenes. All three of them are seen in the photograph above. Foster can been seen in the dark suit in the center of the photograph below. (Both courtesy of Ruth Wischler and Carolyn Wischler McDaniel.)

The British, Chinese, and American cadets stationed at Falcon Field and the Thunderbird Fields were seen in many scenes throughout the movie. (Both courtesy of Ruth Wischler and Carolyn Wischler McDaniel.)

Because the cadets stationed at the Southwest Airways fields were unable to be paid for their work in the movie, as a thank-you, 20th Century Fox built the cadets a swimming pool at Falcon Field. (Above, courtesy of Ruth Wischler and Carolyn Wischler McDaniel; at left, Molly Turner.)

Five

The British are Coming!

The British men who qualified to go to pilot training schools in the United States were sent via ship to Canada, where they hid their British uniforms and donned grey flannel suits. They then boarded trains and scattered across the United States. Some went to California and Florida, others to Texas and Oklahoma. Some came to Mesa, Arizona.

It took a full day to get from Halifax, Nova Scotia, to Moncton, New Brunswick, where there was a holding camp set up where the cadets were sorted out. Trains would then whisk students across the United States on rails such as the Atchison, Topeka, and Santa Fe (ATSF) Railroad through Toronto, Kansas City, St. Louis, and El Paso, or the Chicago, Rock Island, and Pacific Railroad's (CRI&P) *Golden State Limited* through Toronto, Chicago, Tucumcari, and Los Angeles (with a brief stop in Douglas, Arizona, to throw out the cadets).

Sgt. Arthur Graham White (Course 11) related the trip in the *Derby Evening Telegraph*:

> It took five days in all. We lived mainly on hamburgers and coke and whiled away the hours either playing cards (I learned how to play poker on the way) or watching small-town America drift past the carriage windows. We were given no beds on the train. Instead, we had a coach to ourselves, with two seats each, one to sit in and one to put your feet on. You prepared for the night by simply taking off your hat, tie and shoes, rolling up your damp towel to form a pillow and closing your eyes, hoping the rattling train would rock you into unconsciousness. After a couple of sleepless nights, we dismantled our seats and fashioned rough-and-ready beds out of the cushions in the central aisle. On the fifth day we clambered down from our air-conditioned coach into 112 degrees of heat in the shade—only, in Arizona, there was no shade, not in the Sonoran Desert. Like Hansel and Gretel before us, we felt like we had been invited to dinner in an oven.

The cadets chosen for aviation training would gather, like Ken Beeby (far right) and his mates seen above doing in 1942, in towns like Stratford-on-Avon to await transport to Canada. Arriving in Montreal, seen below, they would then travel on to their respective schools. (Above, courtesy of Ken Beeby; below, photograph by Eric Geoffrey Hutchin, courtesy of Catherine Hutchin Harris.)

Ships like the HMS *Letitia* (above) and the SS *Ile de France* (below) transported British troops to Canada for training. The *Letitia* was built at the Fairfield Shipbuilding and Engineering Company shipyards and launched on October 14, 1924. Requisitioned as an armed merchant cruiser, she became a troop ship in 1941 and a hospital ship in 1943 before being returned to civilian service after the war. She was scrapped in 1960. The *Ile de France*, built by Compagnie Générale Transatlantique, was the first major ocean liner to be built after World War I. She was launched on March 14, 1926, at the Penhoët Shipyards and was loaned to the British Admiralty during World War II. Afterward, she returned to civilian service and was also scrapped in 1960, following her last role as a prop in the movie *The Last Voyage* (1960). (Both courtesy of Catherine Hutchin Harris.)

Travel by railway was prevalent in the 1940s. The cadets boarded trains and headed across the United States to their various training schools. The Chicago and Rock Island Express (above) was the first train robbed by Jesse James near Adair, Iowa, in 1873. The Rock Island Diesel Model TA (left) began production in 1937 and had engines of 1,200 horsepower each. (Both photographs by Eric Geoffrey Hutchin, courtesy of Catherine Hutchin Harris.)

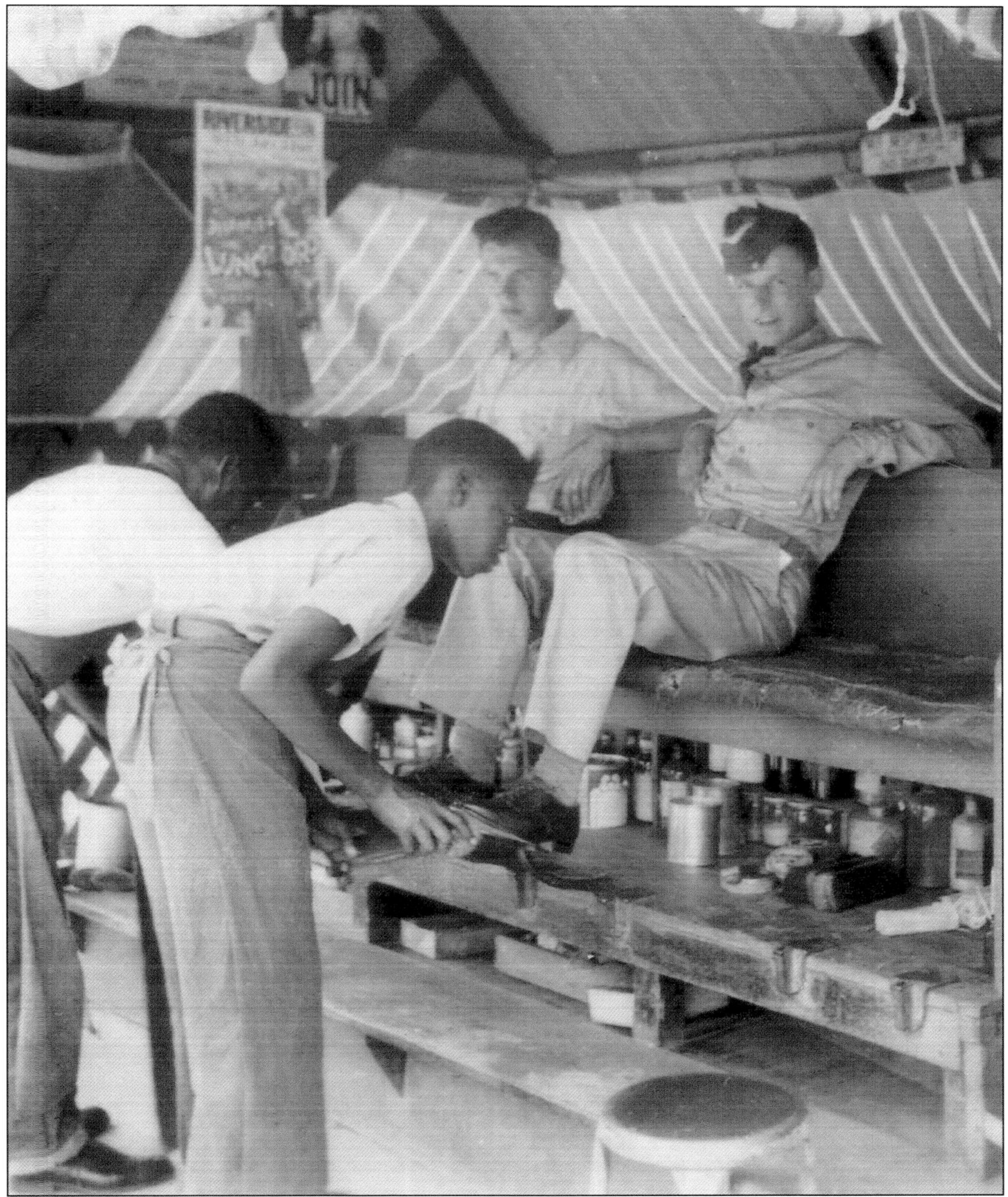

Along the way across the United States, cadets would take in the sights briefly at each stop or take photographs of their friends. In Chicago, Cadet Eric Geoffrey Hutchin (right) and a friend get their shoes shined. (Courtesy of Catherine Hutchin Harris.)

In Tucumcari, New Mexico, Cadets Ken Beeby and Thomas Watt "Jock" Briggs capture the moment on the *Golden State* line before continuing on to Douglas, Arizona. (Courtesy of Ken Beeby.)

The cadets passed through Rock Island City on their way west. As they crossed the Mighty Mississippi River on the Arsenal Bridge, the locks and the Rock Island Centennial Bridge (the arched bridge in the background, built 1938–1940) were visible as they looked north. (Photograph by Eric Geoffrey Hutchin, courtesy of Catherine Hutchin Harris.)

Another stop in Delmar, Iowa, gave the British cadets access to the U.S. Army servicemen traveling throughout the United States for various assignments. (Photograph by Eric Geoffrey Hutchin, courtesy of Catherine Hutchin Harris.)

Union Station, the train depot in Tucumcari, New Mexico, is the only Spanish-style one in the state. The first train arrived in Tucumcari in 1902, but the station that once saw a bustle of activity and thousands of cadets is now mostly abandoned. (Courtesy of Catherine Hutchin Harris.)

Then it was on through the desert to Douglas, Arizona. The El Paso and Southwestern Railroad Depot was an important train station and is considered one of the finest examples of railway architecture of the early 1900s. It was used for transporting copper back east, then soldiers out west. It is now the Douglas Police Station. (Photograph by Eric Geoffrey Hutchin, courtesy of Catherine Hutchin Harris.)

Some of the cadets stopped in at the Grand Canyon. (Both courtesy of Catherine Hutchin Harris.)

If the long trip across the United States was not enough to awe the cadets, the Grand Canyon was the finishing touch. Sgt. Ken Beeby relates, "The U.S. was bigger than anything we could every have imagined or that film could portray." (Photographs by Eric Geoffrey Hutchin, courtesy of Catherine Hutchin Harris.)

Others went to Mexico and took in bullfights and parades. (Both courtesy of Molly Turner.)

They also took pictures of the architecture, in particular El Zócalo, or La Plaza de la Constitución, in Mexico City, which is the third-largest square in the world, after Tiananmen Square in Beijing and Red Square in Moscow. La Catedral Metropolitana sits on the north side and El Palacio Nacional on the south side. The gardens and fountains seen in these photographs from 1943 are now gone. All that remains is a paved square of gigantic proportions and a large Mexican flag on a pole in the center. (Both courtesy of Molly Turner.)

The Westward Ho, when completed in 1927, was the tallest building in Arizona until 1960. It was one of the premier luxury hotels until 1979. Two years later, the 16-story building was converted to housing for senior citizens. This was a popular spot for balls, dances, and parties. The staff and cadets from Falcon Field and the Thunderbird Fields often attend such here. (Photograph by Eric Geoffrey Hutchin, courtesy of Catherine Hutchin Harris.)

Monsoons and dust storms were common at Falcon Field. This dark storm hit the airbase in 1943 and spawned a funnel cloud that missed the airport by 4 miles. (Photograph by Eric Geoffrey Hutchin, courtesy of Catherine Hutchin Harris.)

Palm trees were a new sight for many of the British and Chinese cadets. The ones pictured here grace the property around the Habeeb House, on the southeast corner of the Falcon Field property. (Photograph by Eric Geoffrey Hutchin, courtesy of Catherine Hutchin Harris.)

The main building at Falcon Field, with its tower, was a welcome sight for the road-weary cadets. (Courtesy of Molly Turner.)

Six

The No. 4 British Flying Training School

Falcon Field was not even finished being built when the first group of cadets arrived. But there was no time, and flying commenced on September 14, 1941, nevertheless. The cadets were quickly incorporated into the machine. Half of the day would be spent in classrooms, learning navigation, flight principles, human performance, meteorology, and so on. The other half of the day was spent in the air—first on Stearmans, then on to Vultees and Texans, or, as the British called them, the Harvards. Those who buzzed the city, other bases, or the tower were sent packing.

Navigation instructor H. Dean Page, in the Thunderbird base magazine, wrote about the difficulties of getting into the swing of things, "We all developed into habitual milk drinkers . . . with good reason. It was the only thing we could get. The plumbers were continually testing the water mains. At the most, you could expect a light orange dribble out of the faucets, and ordinarily all you could get would be a momentary gurgle, followed by a dry discouraging hiss."

Classes were held against a backdrop of hammering, sawing, painting, and sawdust. The cadets sat on whatever was available in the barracks during class sessions, or went outside to hold class, while their beds were being painted. Airplanes taxied up and down the runway (though there was no runway, really, just Bermuda grass in an attempt to keep the dust down), side by side with graders, steamrollers, and water trucks.

Courses would consist of approximately 50 men and take 20 weeks of intense primary, basic, and advanced flight and navigation training. After graduation, and a dunk in the pool, it was off to Europe.

Local residents worked at the base as well. In 1941, over 250 civilians were needed to keep the school running, including members, both male and female, of some of Mesa's earliest and prominent families, such as the Bliss, Brimhall, Hamblin, Johnson, LeSueur, Phelp, Rogers, and Wright families. Mary Louise (Turner) Bustrin self-published a book called *My Second Job*, recounting her days in the flight accounting office keeping track of the hours the British pilots spent in the air.

When the cadets were not working, the residents of Arizona would line up at the gates to take them home with them for the weekend, or they would go horseback riding, to the lakes, hiking, or hitchhiking to California.

Upon arrival at Falcon Field, cadets had to check in at the gatehouse and get a photograph taken. The cadet on the left holds a copy of *The Falcon*, the magazine for the base. Meanwhile, trucks carrying supplies move in and out of the front gate, as Bill Fry (driver) does below, with fuel. (Both courtesy of Molly Turner.)

After arrival and checking in at the front gate, cadets would report to their new commanding officer or duty officer. (Courtesy of Molly Turner.)

Squadron leader Stuart Mills (seen here with wife Anne in March 1942) was posted to Washington, D.C., on December 3, 1940, for temporary duty. However, he was named assistant air attaché on February 4, 1941, and was tapped to help select fields and supervise the training of British Royal Air Force pilots in the United States. After flying around the country, critiquing locations at which to build training bases, he served briefly as chief flying instructor at Falcon Field. (Courtesy of Molly Turner.)

Part of cadet training was in the classroom, learning about the principles, procedures, and regulations of flying: navigation, human performance and limitations, flight planning, mass and balance, radio navigation, meteorology, principles of flight, instruments, communications, and more. Then it was on to the flight simulator, or "link trainer," where cadets logged dozens of hours in "virtual reality," though the term was unknown in the 1940s. (Both courtesy of Molly Turner.)

Then it was on to electronics and technical training and on-the-job training of navigation and communications in the tower. Note also the miniature planes dangling from the ceiling below. (Both courtesy of Molly Turner.)

Lectures could occur inside the classroom, in the tower, or out and about the base. Cadets took advantage of every chance to learn something. (Both courtesy of Molly Turner.)

Physical training in the Arizona desert was miserable for most of the British cadets, since they only had six months' at Falcon Field, which was not enough time to acclimatize to the heat. Cadet Eric Hutchin sent a postcard to his parents back in England, dated June 19, 1942, that had the poem "Hell in Arizona" on the front, explaining why the devil hated Arizona. On the back, he wrote, "Dear Mom and Dad, The thing on the other side tells you more than I can, and, anyway, it's too hot to write. I'll send a letter when I get to Phoenix." (Courtesy of Molly Turner.)

Sharpshooting was part of the physical regimen on base. Two cadets try their hand at precision shooting while a trainer looks on. (Courtesy of Molly Turner.)

Stearman Aircraft Corporation was founded in Venice, California, by Lloyd Stearman (1898–1975) in 1927. Four C1 and C2 biplanes were built before Stearman moved the company to Wichita, Kansas, where production of the C3 and Stearman 4 Speedmail were built. In 1929, United Aircraft and Transportation Corporation (UATC) purchased the company but was forced by the Air Mail Act of 1934 to separate its airline and manufacturing operations. Boeing was also spun out from UATC and took Stearman as a subsidiary. The Stearman Model 75, or Kaydet, was first built in the 1930s–1940s as a military trainer aircraft for the U.S. Army Air Force and U.S. Navy. Approximately 40 Stearmans (both PT-17s and PT-17As) were based at Falcon. (Above, photograph by Commanding Officer Marvin R. A. Grant; below, courtesy of Ruth Wischler and Carolyn Wischler McDaniel.)

Nearly 10,000 Kaydets, seen above, were built by Stearman Aircraft Corporation over the lifetime of the product line. Another 40 Stearman PT-13Ds, seen below, arrived in Mesa to replace the original 40 damaged in the August 1945 storm that hit Falcon Field. (Above, courtesy of Molly Turner; below, Rex Griswold.)

North American Aviation (NAA) was founded in 1928 by Clement Melville Keys to be a holding company to buy and sell interests in various airlines and aviation-related companies, but it was forced by the Air Mail Act of 1934 to separate its airline and manufacturing operations (except for Eastern Air Lines, which separated in 1938). General Motors Corporation took a controlling interest the year before and brought James H. "Dutch" Kindleberger (1895–1962) in to run NAA (which was reverse-merged into GM's General Aviation Division) as a manufacturing company. Pictured above are advanced phase instructors offering preflight briefings to cadets. (Above, courtesy of Molly Turner; below, Rex Griswold.)

The T-6 (or AT-6) trainer, called the "Texan" by the Americans and the "Harvard" by the British, was the most widely used trainer ever, with over 15,000 units built by NAA from 1935. Approximately 75 Harvards were based at Falcon. (Above, courtesy of Catherine Hutchin Harris; below, photograph by Sgt. Cy Cartwright, courtesy of Rex Griswold.)

Gerard "Jerry" Vultee and Vance Breese started Airplane Development Corporation (ADC) in early 1932. Soon after, Errett Lobhan Cord bought all 500 shares of stock in the company. Due to the Air Mail Act of 1934, Aviation Corporation (AVCO) established the Aviation Manufacturing Corporation (AMC) through the acquisition of Cord's holdings, including ADC. AMC was liquidated in 1936, and Vultee Aircraft Division was formed as an autonomous subsidiary of AVCO. Vultee acquired the assets of the defunct AMC, including Lycoming and Stinson Aircraft Company. Vultee Aircraft was created in 1939, when Vultee Aircraft Division of AVCO was reorganized as an independent company called the Vultee Aircraft Corporation (VAC). In 1943, VAC merged with Consolidated Aircraft Corporation to form the Consolidated Vultee Aircraft Corporation, or Convair. (Both courtesy of Molly Turner.)

The Vultee BT-13 Valiant was a basic trainer aircraft for the U.S. Army Air Corps/U.S. Army Air Forces. Approximately 20 Valiants were stationed at Falcon Field. In the above photograph, Flight Instructor Bob Hammond (killed in training, January 18, 1943), at right, and Leading Aircraftman Thomas A. Austin (Course 5) are pictured in a BT-13A. (Above, courtesy of Tom Austin; below, Ruth Wischler and Carolyn Wischler McDaniel.)

William "Bill" Sims was the field manager at Falcon Field and an employee of Southwest Airways. (Courtesy of Molly Turner.)

Molly Hurrell was engaged to Flight Lt. Charles Laurence "Laurie" Turner, who had to depart Britain for the United States to work at Falcon Field (January 11, 1943–March 7, 1944). Hurrell came later to the United States (on a flight that included the prime minister of Norway and his family) and married Turner in Coral Gables, Florida, in 1942. She then went to work at Falcon, alongside her husband and other wives and local residents. Some of the Falcon Field RAF staffers were, from left to right, Molly Turner, Lee Harris, Thelma LeSueur, Ruth Marler, and Vera Faulkner. (Courtesy of Molly Turner.)

Before there was wireless cell phone service, before there were cordless phones, before push-button telephones, before rotary dial phones, human hands other than the caller and the call recipient touched every phone call. Telephone exchanges consisted of numerous plug boards staffed by telephone operators, who sat in front of a vertical panel containing banks of jacks, each of which was the local termination of a subscriber's phone line. When a call came through, operators such as Delilah Romine (seen here) had to physically plug a cord into the jack the caller wanted. Falcon Field was no exception. (Courtesy of Molly Turner.)

Feeding a military base was no easy task. There were potatoes to peel, floors to scrub, windows to wash, grease traps to clean out, uniforms to wear, and hair regulations to follow. Here are some of the members of the Falcon Field kitchen staff. (Courtesy of Molly Turner.)

Joe Wischler (1916–1987), on the right, was the chief of maintenance at Falcon Field and kept the planes running with a wicked sense of humor. Once he created a bug sprayer with machine gun sights and ran around eradicating insects. (Courtesy of Ruth Wischler and Carolyn Wischler McDaniel.)

Wischler (fifth from the left), seen here with members of his maintenance staff, was a hands-on boss and was always in the thick of things. According to Jim Dawson's book, *The RAF in Arizona: Falcon Field, 1941–1945*, "If an airplane part did not work, he made a new part. If there was not a tool for the job, he designed and built a tool." (Courtesy of Ruth Wischler and Carolyn Wischler McDaniel.)

Some of Wischler's crew were responsible for washing the planes, others did maintenance, and yet others were responsible for fueling and "resetting" the planes after flight. (Both courtesy of Molly Turner.)

When not working, there was plenty of time to spend on pursuits of leisure. Cadets would relax in the courtyards surrounding the barracks, reading magazines or letters or visiting. They also went horseback riding and felt "really Western." (Both courtesy of Molly Turner.)

Other pastimes included hitchhiking into Hollywood, where many of the cadets would visit with *Thunder Birds* star Gene Tierney (1920–1991) and her husband, Oleg Cassini (1913–2006), or go to the Earl Carroll Theatre. Ken Beeby (Course 11/12) tells of a time when he, Arthur Armin, and Norman Balance (both Course 11) were treated to a ride from Five Points in Phoenix to Hollywood Boulevard in a Buick Straight 8 by a businessman. He also treated the cadets to dinner in Salome along the way and gave them each $5 when he dropped them off. Others would belly up to the bar at the diner on base to share stories. (Above, Catherine Hutchin Harris; below, Molly Turner.)

Besides serving as extras in *Thunder Birds*, the RAF cadets did many other things to promote goodwill in the community and for the war effort. Ken Beeby (Course 11/12, far right) organized some rugby matches in Tucson and Phoenix. Here they pose for a promotional photograph at Thunderbird Field I with cadets from China, Russia, the United States, Canada, and South America. (Courtesy of Ken Beeby.)

Gremlin was the base mascot for a number of years. Someone with a sense of humor put the warning placard on him while he was sleeping and took this photograph. Tragically Gremlin was killed in training in an accident at Falcon Field on May 6, 1943. (Courtesy of Molly Turner.)

There was also time for celebration. Ruth and Joe Wischler dance the night away at the Westward Ho in Phoenix in 1944. (Courtesy of Ruth Wischler and Carolyn Wischler McDaniel.)

El Charro is the oldest Mexican food restaurant in Mesa, having been established in the late 1930s–early 1940s. Cadets and employees from Falcon Field, such as Flight Officer G. R. Coleshill (second to the left), Wing Commander John McKenna (center), Flight Lt. Charles Laurence "Laurie" Turner (second to the right), and Molly Turner (right), found it a favorite hangout location. (Courtesy of Molly Turner.)

Arizona is not known for its tornados, but this funnel cloud approached Falcon Field from the direction of Red Mountain in 1943. It missed the flight deck by 4 miles. Flight Lt. Charles Laurence "Laurie" Turner wrote, "When the meteorological report (which we sent in) said we had a tornado, the authorities would not believe it. But here it is." Falcon Field would not be so lucky two years later when, on August 1, 1945, just a month before the base closed, all of the planes on the tarmac were tossed into the ground or into C. H. McKellips's orange groves. (Photograph by Leading Aircraftman R. Roberts, courtesy of Molly Turner.)

According to Jim Dawson's book, *The RAF in Arizona: Falcon Field, 1941–1945*, the Operations Record Book (ORB) for August 1, 1945 stated, "Began with 'Routine working day.' " This was quickly followed by Flight Lt. Harry Carter's entry, which read, "About 1800 hours a very severe wind storm followed by a dust storm and rain storm occurred, resulting in heavy damage to aircraft." Capt. Marvin Grant added, "[With winds in excess of 60 mph] these planes tried to fly. Every man on the base was out on the flight line, trying to hold the planes down. Many of those tied down were actually flying—in tethered flight. One after the other peeled up and over. They were stacked like Jack Straws across the field and into the citrus grove bordering the west fence line." (Photograph by Flight Instructor David Thiele, courtesy of Ruth Wischler and Carolyn Wischler McDaniel.)

Graduation was always an exciting event for the cadets, full of pomp and circumstance. Arrayed on the tarmac, in front of their Stearmans, Vultees, and Harvards, they would march past the stands to stand in formation before receiving their wings. Guests included Air Marshal Douglas Colyer (1893–1978); Maj. Gen. Ralph P. Cousins (1891–1964), commanding general of the Western Flying Training Command; Group Capt. Henry Alvernon Vickers Hogan (1909–1993), director of flight training; RAF brigadier general Alvan Cleveland Kincaid (1892–1968), commanding general of the American Air Force's 37th Flying Training Wing, and more. (Both courtesy of Molly Turner.)

After graduation, there might be time to have a quiet moment with one's wife or girlfriend for congratulations before each cadet got tossed into the swimming pool in celebration of earning his wings. (Both courtesy of Molly Turner.)

Seven

The Growth of Industry

After the war, many military families, including that of John J. Rhodes, later minority leader of the U.S. House of Representatives, decided to settle in Mesa. Some of the staff and cadets from Falcon also returned. Air-conditioning came into more common use, and tourism also began as a major force in the late 1940s. The decade of the 1950s brought more commerce and industry to Mesa, including early aerospace companies.

The City of Mesa purchased the airport back from the U.S. government under the military surplus provision for $1. Mesa city officials like Virgil Crismon, Rial Randall, and Leonard Sale actively sought tenants for the airfield with an active letter-writing campaign. The Mesa Airport Authority was incorporated in 1951. Jim and Vera Dingman opened the Sunshine Acres Children's Home just north of the airfield on Higley Road.

In June 1957, Bill Talley arranged with the City of Mesa, Arizona, a long-term lease of facilities at Falcon Field, Mesa's small municipal airport, with the stipulation that Talco manage the airport for the city. Construction of the test facilities on the airport property was completed in September of that year. The control tower and an available aircraft hangar became office space and workspace, respectively. Activities involving the small number of aircraft using the airfield were limited to another nearby hangar. Testing of Talco's larger devices was immediately started in Mesa, and by the end of 1957, the drafting and engineering activities began relocating to the Mesa Division. Other future Talley divisions and acquisitions, such as Astro Rocket, Inc., and Rocket Power, Inc., also operated at Falcon.

Until 1960, though, over half of Mesa residents made their money directly or indirectly from farming, mainly citrus and cotton. Beginning in the 1960s, more high-technology companies arrived; health care facilities and medical offices boomed beginning in the 1980s. When the AZ-202 freeway loop finally made it past Higley, another new boom started. Now the Falcon Field Business District comprises over 7,000 acres of space, hosts more than 200 businesses, and employs over 18,000 people.

From 1945 to 1965, the City of Mesa leased the airport property to Franz G. Talley (1919–1973) for his various manufacturing companies. One of them was Rocket Power, Inc. (RPI), founded in 1959 by Charles E. Bartley (1922–1996), developer of the first elastomeric solid propellant at the Jet Propulsion Laboratory (JPL). RPI became part of the Gabriel Company in 1958, which owned Talco Engineering Company, founded by Talley. Talco/Gabriel acquired Bohannon, renamed the entire company Rocket Power, Inc., and sold it to Maremont Corporation. (Courtesy of Falcon Field Airport, City of Mesa.)

A crash test dummy weighted to simulate an average male pilot launches from an airplane in one of Rocket Power, Inc.'s ejection seats in a test near Falcon Field. (Courtesy of Nammo Talley.)

Franz G. Talley founded Talco Engineering in Hamden, Connecticut, manufacturing cartridge-actuated devices used in emergency escape systems for jet-propelled aircraft. He moved the company to Mesa, Arizona, in 1957 before selling the firm to the Gabriel Company. Shortly thereafter, he founded Talley Industries, Inc., which included a subsidiary, Astro Rocket, all located at or near Falcon Field. Eventually, Talley Industries acquired Rocket Power, plus General Time Corporation, General Time Instruments, Electrodynamics, and the Arizona Biltmore Hotel. Talley Defense Systems, Inc., as it was later known, was acquired in 2007 by Nammo AS of Norway and was renamed Nammo Talley. (Both courtesy of Nammo Talley.)

Royal Arabians is a full-service equine facility providing horse stabling, sales and marketing, and performance training. It is just one of numerous horse-related businesses in the area. Nadir Riding Academy is at the same location. Tyler Farms Arabians is located just to the northwest of Falcon Field at the north end of Val Vista Road. Others include Red Mountain Stables and Reproductive Facility, West Wind Stables, and Ilercil Arabians. (Courtesy of Royal Arabians, LLC.)

Citrus Heights Farms is next door to the old Franks house on McDowell Road. (Photograph by author.)

Many new businesses continue to start up or move their operations to Falcon Field. One of the newest arrivals is SolFocus, a leading supplier of solar energy solutions for power plant developers, municipalities, industrial sites and utilities, with headquarters in Mountain View, California. Other recent arrivals include Waxie Sanitary Supply, Sabena Airline Training Center, and Standard Bolt. (Courtesy of SolFocus, Inc.)

Allen Freeman's father, Art Freeman, started farming in Mesa in the 1960s growing cotton, but when the price dropped, he switched to citrus, growing oranges, lemons, and grapefruit. (Courtesy of SRP.)

J&J Materials has been on the southeast corner of the Falcon Field city block since 1969 and actually sits on land that still belongs to the Habeeb family. The company supplies rock, gravel, sand, and other landscaping products that can be found in communities throughout Mesa. (Photograph by author.)

Prism Aviation was one of the mainstay businesses in the airpark in the 1970s. Though gone now, Prism, along with the likes of Marsh Aviation, Tango One Aviation, and other longtime businesses, made Falcon Field a one-stop destination for any and all aircraft needs, from parts to training and sales to overhauls. (Courtesy of Falcon Field Airport, City of Mesa.)

Alliant Techsystems, Inc., (ATK) was founded in 1990 when Honeywell spun off its defense business. For 50 years prior to this, Honeywell supplied defense products and systems to the United States and its allies, including the first electronic autopilot that enabled B-17 aircraft to accomplish pinpoint bombing missions during World War II. ATK expanded into the aerospace market with the acquisitions of Hercules Aerospace Company in 1995 and Thiokol Propulsion in 2001, which transformed the company into the world's largest supplier of solid propellant rocket motors and a leading provider of high-performance composite structures. ATK now is a premier aerospace and defense company with more than 19,000 employees worldwide. (Courtesy of Alliant Techsystems, Inc.)

Heliponents, Inc., encompasses a 40,000-square-foot facility at the Falcon Field airpark and is a full-service fixed-base operator (FBO), including component overhauls, exchanges, aircraft parking, hangar rental space, oxygen and nitrogen service, and more. (Photograph by author.)

In the mid-1980s, Hughes built a facility at the northwest corner of McDowell and Higley Roads, just north of Falcon Field, to manufacture both civilian and military helicopters, including the AH-64 Apache. McDonnell-Douglas (MD) purchased the facility and helicopter line in 1984, which was then acquired by Boeing in 1997 when McDonnell-Douglas merged with Boeing. Now the facility employs more than 4,700 people working on the AH-64 Apache helicopter among its many products. Sen. Barry Goldwater (below) was just one of many dignitaries to speak at the facility since its opening. (Both courtesy of Boeing Company.)

The AH-64 Apache is a four-blade, twin-engine attack helicopter with reverse-tricycle landing gear and a tandem cockpit for two pilots. It was originally built as a Model 77 by Hughes Helicopters for the U.S. Army's Advanced Attack Helicopter Program to replace the AH-1 Cobra. The first Apache saw flight on October 1, 1975. Some of its high-tech features include a nose-mounted sensor suit for target acquisition and night vision systems. It sports a 30-millimeter M230 chain gun between the main landing gear, as well as a combination of AGM-114 Hellfire and Hydra 70 rockets on four hard points mounted on stub-wing pylons. McDonnell-Douglas acquired the aircraft in 1984, and Boeing became the new owner in 1997 when it acquired MD. Apaches are manufactured at the Mesa facility, where over 4,700 employees work. (Both courtesy of Boeing Company.)

AH-64 Apache

Alta Mesa is a master-planned community consisting of approximately 2,600 homes in northeast Mesa that began construction in 1984 just to the east and southeast of Falcon Field. (Photograph by author.)

Singin' in the Rain, based on the 1952 MGM film of the same name, played at the 500-seat Broadway Palm Dinner Theatre in Mesa in February and April 2009. The theater was opened in October 2001 by the Prather Family of Theatres. Their two other properties are the Broadway Palm Dinner Theatre in Fort Myers, Florida, and the Dutch Apple Dinner Theatre in Lancaster, Pennsylvania. (Courtesy of Broadway Palm Dinner Theatre.)

MD Helicopters, Inc., started as the Aircraft Division of Hughes Tool Company in 1955, manufacturing the Hughes 269, 300, 500, 530F, TH-55 Osage, OH-6 Cayuse, and AH-64 Apache. McDonnell-Douglas bought the helicopter business of Hughes in 1984 and, in 1997, merged with Boeing. Two years later, Boeing sold the former MD commercial helicopter business to MD Helicopter Holdings, Inc., which, in turn, was purchased by Patriarch Partners, LLC. Under the direction of Lynn Tilton, MD Helicopters grew its business from 7 to 52 aircraft per year. (Courtesy of MD Helicopters, Inc.)

Longbow Golf Course, named in honor of the Boeing AH-64 Apache Helicopter, was designed by Kenneth M. Kavanaugh, who also designed the Resort at Gold Canyon, Roy Rogers and Dale Evans Happy Trails Resort in Surprise, Quail Creek Country Club in Green Valley, Dell Urich Municipal Golf Course in Tucson, and dozens of others around the country. Construction was completed in 2003. The course also features a 10-foot, 400-pound bronze statue of an archer created by Mesa resident and president of the Mesa Chamber of Commerce Charlie Deaton. (Photograph by Ken Easley, courtesy of Longbow Golf Club.)

Rex and Mary Ellen Griswold opened Anzio Landing at Falcon Field in 1989 and owned and operated the upscale Italian restaurant with panoramic window views of the runways until 2006, when they sold the restaurant to Rich and Susan Cutshall. The restaurant's main focus is on Italian and Mediterranean cuisine. (Courtesy of Rex Griswold.)

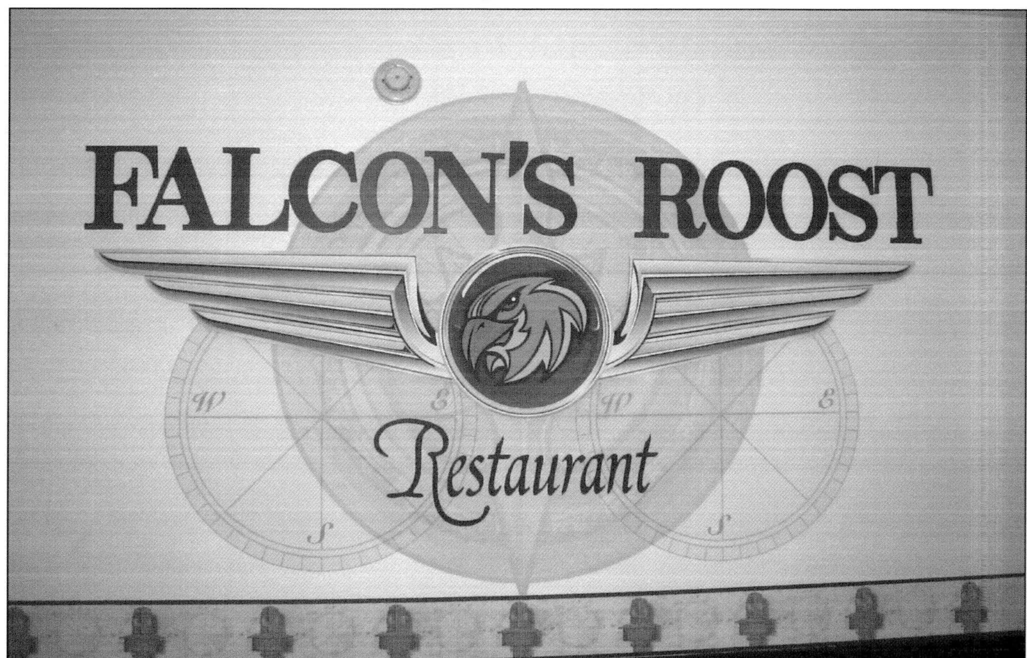

Falcon's Roost Restaurant, once a favorite hangout for pilots, has been through several owners and periods of inactivity. It was reopened in 2008 by Mesa residents Sandy and Veronica Novelli, just north of the Monastery. (Photograph by author, artwork by Gordon Schirling.)

Eight

Airport Operations

Originally opened in 1941 as a pilot training base for Royal Air Force pilots during World War II, Mesa Airport Authority was incorporated in 1951.

However, according to the June 10, 1963, issue of the *Mesa Tribune*, "From the standpoint of an airport, however, Falcon Field didn't really amount to much until a group of local air enthusiasts banded together in the Mesa Aviation Development Association. This group, working in cooperation with the city, the Chamber of Commerce, state and federal aviation officials, Rocket Power, who holds the aviation operations lease as a part of its industrial lease, and whoever else would listen, has stood by until some much needed improvements were pushed through. Completing the job, over the weekend the organization and other groups and agencies staged a dedication program and air show to attract several thousand people to the field so that Mesans would have a better idea of what was out there."

In 1977, the airport created a master plan, laying out a comprehensive analysis of airport needs and alternatives with the purpose of providing direction for future development of the facility. A revision was released in 1992.

Great people have worked at the airport throughout the years, from Bob Bresnahan (1929–1991) and Bernice Cuisinier to Corrine Nystrom and Ernest Hemphill. They have kept things rolling at the airport itself. Meanwhile, Lois C. Yates, executive director of the Falcon Field Area Alliance, and Robert Brown, Otto Shill, and others of the Falcon Field Tenants and Users Association keep business, commerce, and other non-governmental life rolling around the airport proper.

Today Falcon Field Airport is owned and operated by the City of Mesa and is one of the largest airports in the United States in terms of based aircraft and annual aircraft operations. More than 70 businesses are based directly at the airport, and another 130 or so surround the airport in the Falcon Field Business District, including the Boeing Company and MD Helicopters. Falcon Field has over 95 acres of land available for lease and offers competitive lease rates and terms for aviation businesses interested in locating on the airport. It is an airport with historical roots and a vision for the future.

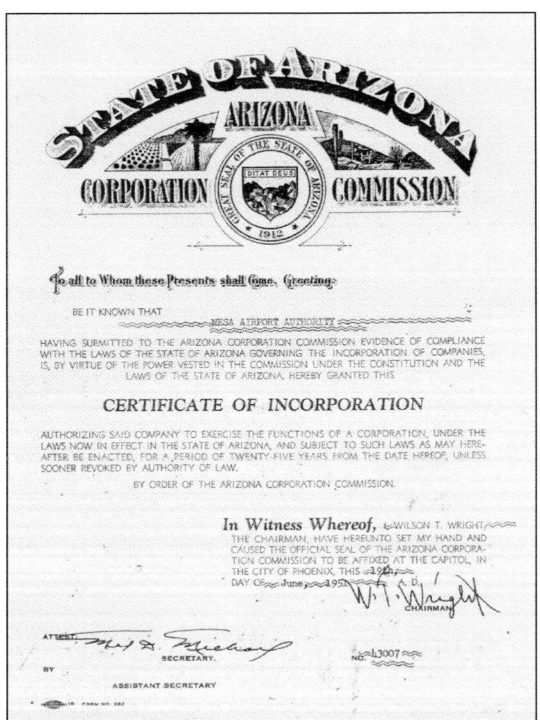

STATE OF ARIZONA
ARIZONA
CORPORATION COMMISSION
GREAT SEAL OF THE STATE OF ARIZONA
DITAT DEUS
1912

To all to Whom these Presents shall Come, Greeting:

BE IT KNOWN THAT MESA AIRPORT AUTHORITY

HAVING SUBMITTED TO THE ARIZONA CORPORATION COMMISSION EVIDENCE OF COMPLIANCE WITH THE LAWS OF THE STATE OF ARIZONA GOVERNING THE INCORPORATION OF COMPANIES, IS, BY VIRTUE OF THE POWER VESTED IN THE COMMISSION UNDER THE CONSTITUTION AND THE LAWS OF THE STATE OF ARIZONA, HEREBY GRANTED THIS

CERTIFICATE OF INCORPORATION

AUTHORIZING SAID COMPANY TO EXERCISE THE FUNCTIONS OF A CORPORATION, UNDER THE LAWS NOW IN EFFECT IN THE STATE OF ARIZONA, AND SUBJECT TO SUCH LAWS AS MAY HEREAFTER BE ENACTED, FOR A PERIOD OF TWENTY-FIVE YEARS FROM THE DATE HEREOF, UNLESS SOONER REVOKED BY AUTHORITY OF LAW.

BY ORDER OF THE ARIZONA CORPORATION COMMISSION.

In Witness Whereof, I, WILSON T. WRIGHT, THE CHAIRMAN, HAVE HEREUNTO SET MY HAND AND CAUSED THE OFFICIAL SEAL OF THE ARIZONA CORPORATION COMMISSION TO BE AFFIXED AT THE CAPITOL, IN THE CITY OF PHOENIX, THIS 19th DAY OF June, 1951 A. D.

W. T. Wright
CHAIRMAN

ATTEST: [signature]
SECRETARY.

NO. 43007

BY
ASSISTANT SECRETARY

FORM NO. 282

On June 19, 1951, the Mesa Airport Authority was incorporated in the state of Arizona. Wilson T. Wright (1918–1973) was the chairman of the Arizona Corporation Commission who signed the company into existence. (Courtesy of Mesa Public Library, City of Mesa.)

Ernest Hemphill was only one of many Mesa residents to work at Falcon Field throughout the decades of its existence. He worked as a security guard at Falcon Field for years. (Courtesy of Falcon Field Airport, City of Mesa.)

These two water towers stood near the swimming pool at Rendezvous Park, a regular hangout place for the British pilots during the 1940s. The short, squat one in the background (right) was built first. The original water tower at Falcon Field was the same shape and nearly the same size as the first Rendezvous Park water tower. It was painted in a red-and-white checkered pattern and disappears from photographs by 1957. The blue bulb tower (below), which still stands today, appeared sometime between 1957 and 1959, based on the aerial photographs. (At right, courtesy of Molly Turner; below, photograph by author.)

The original hangars from the No. 4 British Flying Training School were converted to private plane storage after the closing of the school. (Both courtesy of Rex Griswold.)

Other original buildings from the No. 4 British Flying Training School were converted to other uses after the closing of the school. Superstition Air Service was founded by Chas Harrell and Jim Caldwell. Regulars at SAS included Darrell Greenamyer, Dave Schooled, and Mike Dillon. The company was bought out by Falcon Executive Aviation, Ltd. Miller Aircraft, founded by Pete Miller, is long gone. (Both courtesy of Rex Griswold.)

This aerial picture of Falcon Field, dated 1957, shows what is left of the No. 4 British Flying Training School: the two hangars, the swimming pool, and some outlying buildings. The outline is still visible where the barracks were, around the pool. The photograph is looking southwest. McKellips Road angles up and to the right and bisects Greenfield Road, running down and to the right. The group of buildings visible in the upper right corner, set in the orange groves, is the Franks House, which still exists today, and several other homes that were built by C. H. McKellips for key members of his ranch staff. (Courtesy of Rex Griswold.)

This aerial picture of Falcon Field, dated 1962, shows the new water tower, which, based on other aerial photographs collected during research for this book, appeared sometime between 1957 and 1959. Only one runway existed at this time. Sunshine Acres Children's Home (established in 1954) is located in the upper right corner, with Red Mountain in the background. (Courtesy of Rex Griswold.)

This aerial picture of Falcon Field, dated April 6, 1975, was taken during an air show. A plane can be seen doing aerobatics in the upper left corner just above Sunshine Acres Children's Home. The swimming pool built by 20th Century Fox is visible in the lower right corner. Directly north of the pool are the two original RAF hangars and the control tower. The McDonnell-Douglas plant is not yet built in the northwest corner of McDowell Road and Higley. (Courtesy of Falcon Field Airport, City of Mesa.)

This aerial picture of Falcon Field, dated November 5, 1986, shows more hangars built in the center area as the airport experienced growth. The swimming pool is still visible in Falcon Field Park, near the water tower, but the original RAF control tower between the hangars is gone. The new tower is visible to the northeast of the hangars. To the west, the McKellips orange groves look like computer pixels. McDonnell-Douglas (now Boeing) is to the north of the airport. The empty section just east of MD is where Longbow Golf Club is now, and the buildings to the north of that make up Sunshine Acres Children's Home. Apache Wells (established in 1962) is the community to the east of the airport. (Courtesy of Falcon Field Airport, City of Mesa.)

This photograph shows both the old red-and-white checkered tower (left) and the new tower, built in 1984. (Courtesy of Falcon Field Airport, City of Mesa.)

The Federal Aviation Administration (FAA) built the new air traffic control tower in 1984, when it assumed responsibility for airport traffic control from a private operator that had been operating the tower since before that time. (Courtesy of Falcon Field Airport, City of Mesa.)

A Beechcraft King Air BE-200 twin-engine turboprop is parked in front of the tower at Falcon Field. (Courtesy of Falcon Field Airport, City of Mesa.)

The airport experienced another growth spurt in the 21st century. The Desert Jet Center (the yellow buildings, with McKellips Road in the foreground), built by Falcon 7 LLC and Grubb and Ellis, broke ground on the 14-acre site just to the west of the water tower in 2007. Falcon Field Park is the area surrounded by the oval-shaped road north of the tower. Red Mountain is visible far to the north. The two rounded-roofed buildings behind the water tower are the original hangars from Falcon Field's British training days. (Courtesy of Desert Jet Center.)

The front of the Falcon Field terminal and administrative offices looks much the same today as it did in the 1970s, as evidenced by this photograph. A memorial rock sits just to the right of the front door now, with a commemorative plaque honoring people influential in the development and operation of Falcon Field. Honorees include Wincel F. Pogue (1922–2006), a former pilot and founding member of the Mesa Aviation Development Association (MADA), and Bob Bresnahan (1929–1991), former director of Falcon Field. (Courtesy of Falcon Field Airport, City of Mesa.)

Boomer was the resident airport cat for many years and made himself quite at home in the office. Bernice Cuisinier would put Boomer out the front door and, by the time she got back to her desk, he would have snuck in through the back door and be sitting on her desk. (Courtesy of Falcon Field Airport, City of Mesa.)

Nine

Museums and Shows

There are quite a few museums in and around the area. The Arizona Wing of the Commemorative Air Force (CAF) is an all-volunteer nonprofit 501(c)(3) museum and receives no government funding. The wing is maintained and operated through fund-raising events, gift shop items, and donations. The Arizona Wing members are dedicated to preserving aviation history and wartime memorabilia for future generations. The Arizona Wing's primary mission is to maintain and operate aircraft from World War II to Vietnam. One of their greatest works is the restoration of the *Sentimental Journey*, a B-17G donated by Mike Clarke to the facility.

Champlin Fighter Museum was opened in 1980 in one of the former RAF hangars. It hosted 16 World War I fighter aircraft, including a 1916 Sopwith Pup, and eight World War II aircraft, including a Soviet MiG-21, a 1943 Curtiss P-40N Flying Tiger, and a 1944 Focke Wulf 190. The museum also featured a weapons collection and ran films in the center section of the building. In 2003, the collection was moved to the Museum of Flight in Seattle, Washington, and Doug Champlin moved on to Nevada.

Other local groups that participate in events or hold their own include the Freedom Flyers Aircraft Association (FFAA), Warbirds Unlimited Foundation, Inc., Impala Bob's Classic Car Show, Wings of Flight Foundation, Arizona Pilots Association, First Generation Camaros of Arizona, the Cactus GTO Car Club, Hot Rod Planet Promotions, the Monastery, and more.

Champlin Fighter Museum opened in 1980 in one of the former RAF hangars. It hosted 16 World War I fighter aircraft, including a 1916 Sopwith Pup, the first plane to ever land on an aircraft carrier, and eight World War II aircraft, including a Soviet MiG-21, a 1943 Curtiss P-40N Flying Tiger, and a 1944 Focke Wulf 190. Also featured at the museum was a weapons collection; the Champlin ran films in the center section of the museum. In 2003, the collection was moved to the Museum of Flight in Seattle, Washington. (Courtesy of Falcon Field Airport, City of Mesa.)

The Focke Wulf FW 190, built by a team that included engineer Kurt Tank (1898–1983), was considered by many to be Germany's best fighter plane. The first prototype flew on June 1, 1939, and deliveries to the German Air Force began in late 1940. In 1942, a German deserter gave his FW 190 to the British, which influenced the development of the Hawker Fury and the Folland Fo. 118. (Photograph by and courtesy of Barrett Tillman.)

This aerial picture was taken from a North American SNJ/T-6 Texan of an air show at Falcon Field. This is the same type of plane that was flown by the Royal Air Force cadets at Falcon Field during their training in the 1940s. (Courtesy of Rex Griswold.)

Tempe, Arizona, resident and former pilot Lester Bannick (1911–1993) built this UFO in 1979. Powered by a Volkswagen engine, the UFO was actually flown by Bannick, reaching an altitude of 25 feet. He was arrested on the Gila River Indian Reservation for flying an aircraft without a license. In 1980, it made an appearance at a Phoenix nightclub, rigged to spin around with flashing lights. After the UFO was removed for violating the sign code, Bannick donated it in 1982 to the Freedom Flyers Aircraft Association (FFAA). It sat in a warehouse until 1989, when the late Bob Bresnahan (1929–1991), former director of Falcon Field Airport, and retired pilot Dick Farrington (1922–2006) decided to put it in front of Anzio Landing Restaurant to attract interest in the FFAA and draw customers into the restaurant. (Courtesy of Rex Griswold.)

In 2008, First Generation Camaros of Arizona, the Cactus GTO Car Club, Hot Rod Planet Promotions, and generous citizens and soldiers from around the world formed a charity to help restore the car of a U.S. soldier wounded in Iraq. Over 200 cars were on display on the CAF ramp in front of the museum when Cpl. Jared Foster arrived under the guise of meeting an officer from the Pentagon. Instead, his restored 1968 Chevy Camaro was unveiled to his surprise. The show also raised $7,500 for the Arizona Wing of the Commemorative Air Force to be used on the upkeep of *Sentimental Journey*. (Both photographs by Mike Tribby, courtesy of Lance A. Baker.)

Cpl. Jared Foster, an Arizona soldier wounded in Iraq, stands by his restored 1968 Chevy Camaro at a car show held at the Arizona Wing of the Commemorative Air Force in Mesa. The car was restored secretly by First Generation Camaros of Arizona, the Cactus GTO Car Club, Hot Rod Planet Promotions, and generous citizens and soldiers from around the world as a thank-you to Foster for his service. (Photograph by Mike Tribby, courtesy of Lance A. Baker.)

Warbirds Unlimited Foundation, Inc., is a 501(c)(3) educational foundation based at Falcon Field. The purpose of the group is to educate the public about World War II, honor the men and women who served in the war, and restore aircraft from the conflict. This trio of T6 Texans are the same type of plane the Royal Air Force cadets trained in at Falcon Field in the 1940s. (Courtesy of Arizona Wing, Commemorative Air Force.)

This F4N Phantom II was acquired in November 1988 from the scrap pile at the San Diego Aerospace Museum by the U.S. Navy. Doug Champlin negotiated the rights to display the aircraft at the Champlin Museum. When his collection was sold to the Museum of Flight in Seattle, the Pima Air and Space Museum in Tucson took over the rights to display the plane, which was then loaned to the Arizona Wing of the Commemorative Air Force for display in the Mesa museum. (Courtesy of Arizona Wing, Commemorative Air Force.)

Sentimental Journey was built in 1944 and entered service in the U.S. Army Air Corps on March 13, 1945. Too late to see European action, the plane served in the Pacific Theater for the rest of the war. In 1947, the aircraft came back from Japan and was assigned to Clark Field in the Philippines as a photo-mapping plane, where she served for three years. Then it was on to Eglin Field in Florida, where she worked as a sea rescue craft. (Courtesy of Arizona Wing, Commemorative Air Force.)

Ten

FALCON MEMORIES

K. H. Holmes summed up best what Falcon meant to the cadets in a 1942 issue of *Peregrine*:

> Several months ago—it seems but weeks—we stood, early one morning, in the cold of the Canadian winter and learned that there would be no winter 1941–42 for us, provided we could learn to fly aeroplanes! We were coming to Arizona, to No. 4 B.F.T.S., Mesa, Arizona. Our first reactions to this news were mixed, depending upon which part of America we had set our hearts on being posted to. Some were for Florida, others for California.
>
> To be frank, I did not feel that in Arizona I had drawn a very good horse. "Cactus, cowboys and desert," I thought. (Blame the western films for that!) We really had little idea of what Arizona would be like. Now that we have travelled, and flown, over a considerable part of it, and met some thousands of its population, we like it. Certainly we fully appreciate the term "Western hospitality!"
>
> Much good has been done by contact between this small English settlement and the residents of the Valley of the Sun. Each has learned to appreciate the good points of the other, and to understand those small differences which each are bound to have.
>
> We have been asked if we are looking forward to going back to England. Our answer, "Yes," somewhat surprises many of our friends. How could we want to go back from a peaceful valley to the war front, from plenty of food to rationing, from sunshine to fog? It is not so easy to answer unless the listener can appreciate that we came here to learn to fly, to do a job which (we hope) will help toward winning the war.
>
> One of the big principles involved in this war is the continuance of family life as we in England and America have learned to appreciate. There you have the reason why we want to return "home." Of course there are exceptions, for some of our number managed to leave their hearts on the thorn of a cactus as they wandered in the desert. . . . Some of us will, I am sure, return here after the war, if ever the pocket allows it. Others will settle here. Now, however, it is "So long, Arizona."

The cadet lounge at Falcon Field was a place to hang out after training, visit with friends, and tell stories. In this photograph, taken during the war years, a flight navigator (evidenced by the single upswept wing on his breast) spins yarns for the cadets. (Courtesy of Molly Turner.)

The chimney is all that is left of the cadet lounge. It still stands in Falcon Field Park, just south of the two original hangars—one of the last remnants of the Royal Air Force training base. A commemorative plaque on it reads, "This fireplace & chimney are part of the building which served as the cadet lounge when Falcon Field was operated as No. 4 British Flying Training School in the years 1941–1945." (Photograph by author.)

Many of the cadets who trained at Falcon Field during war paid the ultimate price. Their graves are scattered across four continents. Flight Lt. Eric Geoffrey Hutchin (Course 10, June 23, 1942–January 1, 1943) was killed in action on April 12, 1945, when his plane was shot down over Germany. He is buried at Becklingen War Cemetery in Germany (right). Flight Lt. Robert Charles Platt (Course 5, November 2, 1941–May 3, 1942), son of James Francis and Amelia Louisa "Minnie" Platt of Teddington, Middlesex, England, was killed in action on July 4, 1943, when his BK718 was lost over Germany. Six of the seven crew members were killed, and the rear gunner was taken prisoner by the Germans. Platt is buried at Overloon War Cemetery in the Netherlands (below). (At right, photograph by and courtesy of Catherine Hutchin Harris; below, courtesy of Commonwealth Graves Commission.)

Twenty-three Royal Air Force cadets, one American cadet, and four instructors were killed during training at Falcon Field. They are LAC: Alexander Thomas Brooks, Paul Cecil John Colling, Alec Henry Sutton, Peter Duncan Campbell, William Burke, Frank Glew, Jack Payne, Harold Edward Hartley, William James Watters, Robert Lawther, Horace Raymond John Partoon, George Davison, James Gilliam Buchanan, Robert Brotherton Horn, John Going Versturme-Bunbury, Walter William Chamberlain, Arthur Roydon Lewis, John Reginald Durston, and Anthony Simpson Lovett; F/I: Bob Hammond, Barney John Gordon, Willard W. Schendel, James Earl Netser, and Donald Walker; A/C: Lawrence A. Janson; AC2/C: Albert Morris, and Peter Frederick Mitson; Corporals Reginald George Henry Clarke and John Leopold Gomm. They repose with honor, with several of their colleagues who have since died of natural causes, in the Mesa City Cemetery. Each year, the Falcon Field Association and the Daughters of the British Empire hold a memorial service to honor their fallen comrades. Past dignitaries included Gen. Jimmy Stewart, various mayors of Mesa, and governors of Arizona. After their deaths many years later, Wing Commander John McKenna and Flight Lt. Norman Dibble both had their ashes scattered across Falcon Field. (Both photographs by author.)

Though many of the cadets from Falcon Field paid the ultimate price, happier events have occurred regularly since World War II. On May 28, 2001, U.S. president George W. Bush signed the World War II Memorial Bill at the White House and laid a wreath on the Tomb of the Unknown Soldier at Arlington National Cemetery before flying to Mesa, where he gave a speech paying tribute to veterans at the Champlin Fighter Aircraft Museum. (Both courtesy of Falcon Field Airport, City of Mesa.)

Carl Jensen, one of the cofounders of Forever Living Products, began building Stonebridge Manor in 1979 as a private residence; it was completed in 1981. The Jensens lived in the 16,000-square-foot, 10-bedroom, 14-bathroom home (complete with two kitchens, two laundry rooms, a movie theater, a 150-foot hallway, and secret passages) until 1985. It then became office space until the late 1980s. A retired schoolteacher bought the property and lived in it, intending to open a bed-and-breakfast, until 1996. In 1998, Michael Mills and Jim Flake bought the property and, after extensive redesign and remodeling, opened Stonebridge Manor as a wedding facility. (Photograph by and courtesy of Roberta Esch.)

On December 29, 2005, the author, Daryl Mallett, and his wife, Barbara, were married in a 16th-century French wedding at Stonebridge Manor. From left to right are Ethan Moe, Shannon Dempsey, Tricia Biggs, Barbara (Biggs) Mallett, Daryl Mallett, Catherine Biggs, Cody Barker, and Brendan Maclear. (Photograph by Carole Dempsey, courtesy of Shannon Dempsey.)

Founded in 1941 as the No. 4 British Flying Training School, Falcon Field Airport is now owned and operated by the City of Mesa. It is home to over 900 aircraft and boasts an industrial park with over 30 aviation-related business and 50 commercial enterprises. It is now the third-largest airport in Arizona and is one of the busiest airports in the United States in based aircraft and annual aircraft operations, and it is a few hundred yards south of the 202 Freeway Loop in Northeast Mesa. (Above, courtesy of Falcon Field Airport, City of Mesa; below, photograph by author.)

Consistent with our mission to preserve history on a local level, this book was printed in South Carolina on American-made paper and manufactured entirely in the United States. Products carrying the accredited Forest Stewardship Council (FSC) label are printed on 100 percent FSC-certified paper.